T0304780

# Closing the Care Gap
# with Wearable Devices

Patient-focused healthcare, driven by COVID-19 experiences, has become a hallmark for providing healthcare services to patients across all modalities of care and in the home. The ability to capture real-time patient data, no matter the location, via remote patient monitoring, and to transmit that data to providers and organizations approved by the consumer/patient, will become a critical capability for all healthcare providers. Of all the remote patient monitoring product designs, wearable medical devices are emerging as the best positioned to support the evolving patient-focused healthcare environment.

This book is for those who are evaluating, selecting, implementing, managing, or designing wearable devices to monitor the health of patients and consumers. This book will provide the knowledge to understand the issues that mitigate the risk of wearable technologies so people can deliver successful projects using these technologies. It will discuss their use in remote patient monitoring, the advantages and disadvantages of different types of physiological sensors, different wireless communication protocols, and different power sources. It will describe issues and solutions in cybersecurity and HIPAA compliance, as well as setting them up to be used in healthcare systems and by patients.

# Intelligent Health Series

**Closing the Care Gap with Wearable Devices**
*Innovating Healthcare with Wearable Patient Monitoring*
Michael W. Davis, Michael J. Kirwan, Walter N. Maclay and
Harry P. Pappas
2023

**Leveraging Technology as a Response to the COVID Pandemic**
*Adapting Diverse Technologies, Workflow, and Processes to Optimize
Integrated Clinical Management*
Paul H. Frisch and Harry P. Pappas
2023

# Closing the Care Gap with Wearable Devices

## Innovating Healthcare with Wearable Patient Monitoring

Edited by
Michael W. Davis
Michael J. Kirwan
Walter N. Maclay
Harry P. Pappas

Routledge
Taylor & Francis Group

A PRODUCTIVITY PRESS BOOK

First published 2023
by Routledge
605 Third Avenue, New York, NY 10158

and by Routledge
4 Park Square, Milton Park, Abingdon, Oxon, OX14 4RN

*Routledge is an imprint of the Taylor & Francis Group, an informa business*

*Library of Congress Cataloging-in-Publication Data*
A catalog record for this book has been requested

ISBN: 978-1-032-30231-7 (hbk)
ISBN: 978-1-032-30230-0 (pbk)
ISBN: 978-1-003-30403-6 (ebk)

DOI: 10.4324/9781003304036

Typeset in Garamond
by Apex CoVantage, LLC

# Dedication of This Book

### Michael W. Davis—Author, Researcher and Editor

I would like to dedicate this book to my wife Marilyn, who has tolerated me for 48 years! I also dedicate this book to my dear friend and business partner for over 15 years, David Garets, who passed away this year.

### Michael J. Kirwan—Author, Researcher and Editor

To my children, Gavin and Ella, who will certainly benefit from the great knowledge found within this book. To my beautiful wife Wendy, my contribution to this book would not have been possible without her inspiration, support and patience. She has literally saved my life many times over.

There are also many friends and family whom I've leveraged to validate portions of this book. I'm grateful that they've remained friends throughout my continuous distraction to make this process and, finally, this book a reality. I've greatly appreciated working closely with Harry, Walt, and Mike in making this book possible and meeting with the other authors of this book before, during and after (hopefully) Covid-19.

### Walter N. Maclay—Committee Chairman

To my wife, Lydia, and all the dedicated employees of Voler Systems, who satisfy customers every day by creating great devices. I also want to thank the others on this page, who made this book possible after a great deal of work.

### Harry P. Pappas

I would like to thank and dedicate this book not only to my immediate family but also to my extended family who helped put this book together. I thank my team of authors and editors and Walter N. Maclay, Chairman of our Wearables Book team and President of Voler Systems. Walt is a global leader in the design and manufacturing of wearable devices with firsthand knowledge of wearable devices; Michael J. Kirwan, my longtime friend in the www.IEEE.org organization and an expert in medical device standards and all things mobile. Also, I need to include my associate in crime, Michael W. Davis, one of the most knowledgeable people that I know in wearable technologies. And I survived as one of the editors and organizers of the book.

I would be remiss if I did not thank and acknowledge the hidden contributions that my wife, Linda, has made on this and many other projects along the many years of marriage to a wild entrepreneur, along with my children, Mark Pappas and Maria Pappas Sparling; my daughter-in-law, Giorgia Meseti Pappas; my son-in law, Steve Sparling; along with my grandchildren, Penelope and Giada Pappas, for their support as I worked on this book so that others may learn and unlearn about the world of wearables and their impact on telehealth.

# Contents

# Series Preface

The Intelligent Health Association (IHA) is pleased to be publishing a series of educational books under the name of the "Intelligent Health Series" in cooperation with our publisher, Taylor & Francis, a division of Informa, a publicly traded, London-based global events corporation.

The IHA advisory board and the IHA Educational committee have identified experts in many areas of health and wellness and have formed several committees, comprised of healthcare professionals and technology thought leaders, for the purpose of publishing a set of technology-centric books for the health and wellness community.

This book is for wearable device manufacturers, health and wellness telehealth professionals, and clinicians, along with those who are involved in the research, design, and manufacturing of medical devices that are mobile and worn on your body or embedded technology woven into shoes and apparel.

For this book, we organized a team of wearable device and telehealth experts to both author and edit chapters in this book.

The publication of this book and others will be available online via Barnes & Noble, Amazon, etc. Content from the books will also be repurposed into audiobooks, podcasts, webinars, and conferences in cooperation with its editors and authors.

Prior books sponsored under IHA's leadership and its partners have been well received and circulated internationally. For example:

www.amazon.com/Voice-Technology-Healthcare-Leveraging-Experiences/dp/0367403862/ref=sr_1_1?crid=3U7A0ZQY9YPGA&dchild=1&keywords=voice+technology+in+healthcare&qid=1599062738&sprefix=Voice+technologies+in+healthcare%2Caps%2C165&sr=8–1

This and other books in the Intelligent Health Series will be marketed through future conferences promoted by IHA and its partners, through Wikipedia, LinkedIn, and various industry and training events worldwide where IHA participates.

Let's educate the global health and wellness community together.
Thank you and enjoy reading this book; your comments are welcome.

**Harry P. Pappas, Editor**
Founder and CEO
Intelligent Health Association

# Preface

Remote monitoring of individuals through connected health devices encompasses capturing and securing data in dynamic mobile environments outside of the clinical environment: such as the tracking, storing and forwarding of a person's vital signs data and their measurement time-stamps as they travel over different time zones, within environments with no or poor connectivity and in instances of an abrupt loss of connectivity or power. This includes protecting and securing a person's privacy while ensuring responsiveness of concerns encountered during the monitoring of their data.

Achieving medical-grade interoperability means: multiple sensor types of data, e.g., vital signs sensor data from a glucose monitor, a blood pressure cuff, a pulse-oximeter, thermometer or any other remote monitoring device, may be sent separately or combined as multi-measurements and be clearly understood by healthcare providers and the care support systems they use end-to-end—all the while the context of the data remains. Healthcare providers have an authentic and holistic view and understanding of the data because the chemical, biological and medical science data is understood through its comprehensive nomenclature coding system, as per widely used standards.

The data model can accommodate the needs of use cases across the healthcare system, so deployments can handle data that serve the most demanding Use Cases in this respect. Other deployments may work with simpler subsets as appropriate. This is to accommodate care scenarios that involve complex hospital treatment as well as scenarios that do not, like prevention programs. As an example, for an ICU patient there is much more relevant data to "blood pressure" than for a general practitioner visit.

Time order of measurements is preserved regardless of poor connectivity conditions that occur from time to time and the individual moving between time zones (and possibly switching between home and travel measurement devices).

Privacy and security provisions as well as authentication of the individual and the devices meet the legal and other needs of the healthcare sector. Interoperability between devices, gateways and services has been achieved through harmonization with existing adopted healthcare standards and protocols understood by regulatory agencies, governments, EHRs, clinicians, etc. and as validated with the muster and rigor of a globally accepted conformity acceptance scheme requiring the very best practices for compliance and interoperability.

To achieve this, the Continua Design Guidelines (CDG), now a part of the IHE Technical Framework, achieves medical-grade interoperability by specifying an end-to-end information and communication technology (ICT) framework for personal connected health solutions based on recognized open standards, to create a secure and interoperable health data exchange. They enable the secure flow of medical-grade data among sensors, gateways and services by providing clear guidance on their interoperability by adding the necessary missing features within the underlying standards or specifications. The value that the CDG provides is secure medical data exchange fully harmonized with existing adopted healthcare standards and protocols understood by regulatory agencies, governments, EHRs, clinicians, etc.

As a result, medical-grade data is both generic and extensible. This was the core tenet of the Continua Design Guidelines (CDG) envisioned in 2006 by Continua Health Alliance: to foster the integration of medical-grade health/sensor data to flow from a multitude of vital signs devices used by consumers to health services, all the way into local, regional or national EHRs and data lake services in a safe and secure manner. Compared to other data models, where there is a different structure defined for every measurement type (such as Bluetooth LE, Open mHealth and many proprietary models), Continua's data model has an extensible structure composed of: a limited set of physiological measurements (where only the Type, Value, Unit and Timestamp are required), and clearly defined attributes that efficiently describe and model hundreds of different health/sensor measurement types (i.e., Temperature, Glucose, Blood Pressure, Insulin Pump, CGM, Fitness, with many more clearly specified codes that define the science of each type as determined by the medical community).

The CDG's medical-grade data model is analogous to FHIR (Fast Health Interoperability Resources) in that it defines a small set of base types that can be used to model more complex devices. The Continua approach supports a dynamic and scalable ecosystem—something that is untenable with other existing data models. This means that gateway developers (computer and mobile app developers) who implement the CDG data model won't need to update their product coding over time in order to handle different measurement types sent from another vendor's Continua-compliant device— the gateway will always work. And through the CDG, all of this maps directly into the HL7 record set: including version 2, version 3 and now HL7 FHIR. This allows for easy and uniform transcoding to legacy systems without loss or distortion of clinical meaning.

# Editors

**Michael W. Davis**

Mike has over 40 years of experience in healthcare and healthcare IT. He completed graduate degrees in clinical pathology and clinical research at the University of Nebraska, and in business administration at Pfeiffer University. Mike held executive management positions at Gartner, HIMSS Analytics, Advisory Board Company, and Mountain Summit Advisors. Mike has been an independent consultant since 2013, advising domestic and global companies on healthcare strategies and acquisitions.

**Michael J. Kirwan**

Vice President of Certification and Standards, LoRa Alliance

Michael drives the intellectual curiosity of LoRa Alliance's certification and standards development. With over 25+ years of introspective experience driving international certification and open standards development, he has helped to lead several alliances to success, such as the Bluetooth SIG, Continua Health Alliance, PCHAlliance, HIMSS, IEEE and is now fully committed to doing the same for LoRa Alliance.

Professionally, he has worked daily with IoT technical, test and certification groups, regulatory, security, policy groups and thought leaders in open standards worldwide as a staff member, a chair and a devoted key stakeholder. Michael holds an MBA from the University of North Carolina, a BS in Industrial Engineering and Technology from Northwest Missouri State University, is PMP certified (Program Management Professional) and recognized as a Bluetooth Qualification Consultant (BQC) and Continua Certified Expert (CCE) and aspires to be such an expert in LoRaWan in the coming years.

Personally, he is a pilot, a magician, a 2nd degree Taekwondo Blackbelt and is passionate about helping people succeed.

**Walter N. Maclay**

Walter N. Maclay, President and Founder of Voler Systems, is committed to delivering quality electronic products on time and on budget. Voler Systems provides integrated design, development and risk assessment of new devices and specializes in the design of wearable devices. He has led Voler Systems to become one of the top electronic design firms in Silicon Valley. Voler Systems is especially well-known for the design of sensor interfaces, wireless, motion control and medical devices. The company has developed medical devices, wearable devices, home health products and products for the aging.

Mr. Maclay is recognized as a domain expert in Silicon Valley technical consulting associations. He has spoken on sensors, wearable devices, wireless communication and low-power design. From 2008 to 2010, he was President of the Professional and Technical Consultants Association (PATCA). He is a senior life member of the Institute of Electrical and Electronic Engineers (IEEE) and a member of the Consultants Network of Silicon Valley. He has been an instructor at Foothill College in the Product Realization Certificate Program, teaching successful new product introduction skills. He has applied his outstanding leadership to many multidisciplinary teams that have delivered quality electronic devices. Mr. Maclay holds a BSEE degree in Electrical Engineering from Syracuse University.

Mr. Maclay is active in helping technology startup companies. He has participated in angel investor groups and has advised dozens of startup companies on technical and funding issues. He has mentored startups at Techstars and Cleantech Open. He is a reviewer for NSF SBIR grants. As founder of his own company, he has dealt with issues of funding, product development, marketing, sales and finance, giving him the experience to advise others. Voler Systems is a member of a technology consortium, the Product Realization Group, which provides all the services to introduce new technology products. Mr. Maclay started and led two forums for CEOs of small companies to discuss issues of importance to them.

**Harry P. Pappas**

Pappas is a successful high-tech serial entrepreneur with a strong focus on the health technology sector. He is a strong believer in applying technology to transform the health and wellness community in today's "Continuum of care" from the hospital to the primary care giver and to the patient's Smart Home. Pappas firmly believes that the world of digital health is being driven by the adoption of technology and therefore the need for quality, ONGOING education.

Harry is a global thought leader and has been a tech geek since the age of 12. He is a speaker at many health and wellness conferences and trade shows around the world.

He and his team are the producers of the award-winning "Intelligent Health Pavilion" ™, a technology-centric DIGITAL HOSPITAL that you may have visited at many trade shows around the world, including at HIMSS over the last 10 years.

Pappas is the Founder and CEO of the Intelligent Health Association, a global social purpose, educational and technology-centric organization dedicated to helping educate members of the healthcare community on the adoption of new technologies, new software, smart drugs, apply digital therapeutics and apps that can improve patient care, patient outcomes and patient safety, while driving down the cost of healthcare.

Harry is also the creator of the i-HOME™, an "In Context" concept that demonstrates a plethora of health and wellness technologies placed in a Digital Smart Home setting. Harry was developing the concept of the "Smart Home" utilizing Steve Jobs' original Apple "NEWTON" PDA device many years ago.

He is an "outside the box" thinker and a long-term strategic player in the world of health technologies for the digital hospital and for today's Smart Home.

Harry is unique in that he has hands-on experience with a wide variety of technology and software development projects as they relate to the health and wellness industries. He has been ahead of the technology curve most of his life and was developing data-driven e-commerce websites back in 1994.

Harry is an internationally recognized thought leader with auto-ID, BLE, NFC, RFID, RTLS, Sensors, Voice, Robotics and Wireless technologies. He has been presenting educational programs around the world since 2001.

Harry's Goal: To help educate the healthcare community on an ongoing basis so that it may adopt new technology, software, apps, Voice, 5G, Blockchain and AI that can have a dramatic impact on the delivery of improved health.

Mantra: "Help Others" and Do "SOCIAL GOOD"

# Contributors

**Audrey Arbeeny** Audrey Arbeeny is CEO and Executive Producer of Audiobrain, founded in 2003, widely recognized as global leaders in sonic branding. Audiobrain's iconic sonic branding initiatives include Microsoft's Xbox 360, Google, Holland America Line, IBM, KIA Motors Corp, GlaxoSmithKline, Microsoft, Merck, Bayer Healthcare, Johnson and Johnson, Logitech, Whirlpool, Toshiba, Major League Soccer and many others.

In addition to music and branding expertise, Audrey has significant backgrounds in psychology, biomusicology and psychoacoustics, and conducts research in these areas. Health and science have long been a part of Audrey's studies and professional discipline, and Audiobrain leads many sonic branding initiatives based around health and wellness through the intentional development of music, sound, voice and vibration experiences, ranging from heart/heath wearables to surgical robotics.

She has been Music Supervisor for 10 Olympic Broadcasts with NBC, for which she has received two Emmy Awards. With over 25 years of specializing in sonic branding, Audiobrain is at the forefront of emerging technologies, and their sonic imprints are heard millions of times a day throughout the world.

An accomplished musician, Audrey lectures on sonic branding at Pratt Institute and is a visiting lecturer and mentor of the Masters in Branding Program at the School of Visual Arts, and is an Adjunct Professor at the Fashion Institute of Technology. She has appeared in many publications, podcasts and has authored must-read articles on the use of intentional music, sound and voice.

Professional affiliations include the National Academy of Television Arts and Science, The Recording Academy, Guild of Music Supervisors and Design Management Institute. Publications include Design Management Institute's *Design for a Holistic Customer Experience*. Audrey has been featured in many publications, including *Fast Company, Variety, The New York Times, Ad Age, The Atlantic* and *The Times UK*. She is a contributing author to the book *The Voice of Healthcare.*

Sonic Branding Speaking Engagements include Harvard Medical School, Advertising Week, CES 2020, Alberta College of Art and Design, Project Voice and Thunderbird School of Global Management. Audrey has been featured on many podcasts, including *This Week in Voice*, The *Voice of Healthcare, FUSE calls, Design Matters with Debbie Millman, Voicebot AI* and many more. She is a member of the Open Voice Network

**Chris Landon MD, FAAP, FCCP, FRSM** When Dr. Landon founded LPF in 1992, he set out to improve the lives of children and their families in Ventura County and beyond.

Dr. Christopher Landon has been Director of Pediatrics at Ventura County Medical Center since 1989. Although it has taken longer than he planned, this has allowed the building of the Pediatric Diagnostic Center to serve the pediatric subspecialty care needs of the Central Coast, including CCS Specialty Care Centers in Endocrinology, Neurology, Ophthalmology, Cleft Lip and Palate and Gastroenterology. He has been involved in telemedicine for as long, building out the first Blue Cross Telemedicine project. The Landon Pediatric Foundation (LPF) built out the first pediatric hospitalist service, Pediatric Intensive Care Unit, state funding to rebuild the Pediatric Unit and a Ronald McDonald Family Living Center. Working with the community LPF has built camps, Moms and Kids Drug Recovery Centers, and established early developmental screening, literacy and education. Working with Dr. Paul Russell, Dr. Landon established Healthy Families Ventura over two and a half decades ago. The Family Justice Center, our partners in ACES, is key to its sustainability. After "retiring" from the role of Director of the Pediatric Diagnostic Center in 2017, Dr. Landon has been able to return to clinical innovation with medical devices with current projects in ventilators, airway clearance, noninvasive pulmonary function testing, advanced mask protection, medication adherence, etc. TV and podcast production has continued through GetMovingTV on YouTube. Through Landon Pediatric Foundation, Dr. Landon continues to pursue Global Health with partners in Africa, Latin America and Australasia.

Dr. Landon enjoys off-road bicycling and practices self-care by painting, gardening, raising bees, butterflies and chickens, cooking, laughter yoga, motorcycles, music, writing and communicating with friends.

**Esvyda** Provider of remote patient monitoring services to health providers. The following contributed to the chapter.

**Simon F. Meza,** Marketing and Sales Manager, has skills and knowledge in organizational competitiveness, with more than four years of experience in marketing and customer support. Abilities to interpret and understand the dynamics of the environment and propose alternatives based on management, research, planning, communication and negotiation.

**Elias Lozano,** CEO, Esvyda, a highly motivated technical/business leader in digital healthcare IT technology development, both in software and system architecture generation. Co-architected Esvyda Software-as-a-service IoT platform.

**Adrian Alexander,** VP of Sales, specializes in Sales and Marketing of Medical Devices, Telehealth Initiatives, IT Consulting and Data management, Financial Accounting, Insurance, Travel Industry and Customer Care.

**Paola Bonilla,** VP Business Development and Sales, has more than 10 years of experience and knowledge in Business, Marketing, Human Resource Management and Sport Science focused on technology and industry sectors.

**Wilson Jaramillo,** VP of Engineering, has more than 10 years of experience in the construction of databases, information systems and web platforms. Currently focused on software architecture and leading projects for digital healthcare IT Technology, Industrial Telemetry and IoT solutions.

**Laurie M. Orlov** Laurie M. Orlov, a tech industry veteran, writer, speaker, and elder care advocate, is the founder of *Aging and Health Technology Watch*, which provides market research, trends, blogs and reports that provide thought leadership, analysis and guidance about health and aging-related technologies and services that enable boomers and seniors to sustain and improve their quality of life. In her previous career, Laurie spent many years in the technology industry, including nine years at analyst firm Forrester Research. She has spoken regularly and delivered keynote speeches at forums, industry consortia, conferences and symposia, most recently on the business of technology for boomers and seniors. She advises large organizations as well as non-profits and entrepreneurs about trends and opportunities in the age-related technology market. Her segmentation of this emerging technology market and trends commentary have been presented in the Journal of Geriatric Care Management. Her perspectives have been quoted in *Business Week*, CNBC, *Forbes*, *Kiplinger*, NPR, *The Wall Street Journal* and *The New York Times*. She has a graduate certification in Geriatric Care Management from the University of Florida and a BA in Music from the University of Rochester. Advisory clients have included AARP, Argentum, Microsoft, Novartis, J&J, United Healthcare, CDW Healthcare, Bose, Cox Communications and Philips. Her latest reports include the *2021 Market Overview of Technology for Aging, The Future of Remote Care Technology and Older Adults 2020, Voice, Health and Wellbeing 2020* and *The Future of Voice First Technology and Older Adults* (2018). Laurie has been named one of the Top 50 Influencers in Aging by Next Avenue and one of the women leading global innovation on Age Tech.

# CURRENT AND FUTURE USES OF WEARABLE DEVICES

**1**

# Chapter 1

# A Diabetic's Story of Wearable Technology: A Spider Bites— Now You're a Type 1 Diabetic

Michael J. Kirwan

How can this happen? I was bitten, but certainly don't feel like Spider-Man. I am 49 years old; lean and physically fit for my entire life; healthy and never any chronic issues, ever. Then, one day like any other in early summer, suddenly pain strikes. Initially a bite-like thing occurred on my left shoulder while I was sitting in a chair outdoors at a resort in south Missouri. I recall immediately jumping up from the wrought-iron chair I was sitting in and looking for whatever it was that stung me. My first thought was a spider bite, but despite a careful search I never found the culprit.

The very next day, my left foot was so sensitive I could not walk without extreme pain. For the next week I was to lead a group of 22 Cub Scouts at a day camp in Kansas, so I suffered through the camp with the sore foot. This was also a week of very high heat outdoors, which required lots of hydration for the scouts (and me) via Gatorade, lemonade, Kool-Aid, water and sodas—so tons of sugar carbs. Not a good concoction for a soon-to-be-diagnosed Type 1 diabetic. At the end of each day, I could barely function; I had nearly zero energy and succumbed to napping for hours after each day of camp—I rarely ever napped. By the end of the week, my wife, a nurse, recognized that I needed urgent medical attention and set up an emergency appointment with my primary doctor. A urine test later indicated my glucose

DOI: 10.4324/9781003304036-2

3

level was four times normal (normal is 80 to 100 mg/dl; I was over 400), so I was immediately admitted to the hospital. I spent the next four days in the hospital being diagnosed by many doctors, including infectious disease, endocrinologists, and other specialists. The outcome was that I had experienced an autoimmune event that essentially killed my pancreas (the insulin-producing organ), so I was diagnosed as a Type 1 diabetic who was now fully dependent on frequent daily insulin injections.

Wow! Before this, I had no real understanding of what diabetes really was, let alone the differences between type 1 vs. type 2 or other types. Realization set in. I've lost a vital organ. How can you live without a vital organ? You can't, right? But you can! If you have the ability to manage your glucose levels continuously using technology and medicine, you can prolong your life in an almost normal way (more specifically—your quality of life—so you can potentially live a full life). Holy s*#t, what a relief—I can get through this if I can learn to continuously manage my diabetes! But how?

My story may be a bit odd; spiders don't cause diabetes, but people with diabetes or with any other chronic illness can learn to scientifically manage and monitor the effects of their disease using technology and the right therapy. And in many cases, they can do it mostly on their own, remotely as they live their life. In my case, at the time I was diagnosed, the main therapy was via use of a small glucose meter which required pin-pricking my fingers several times per day and placing a blood sample into the meter via a strip, which then gave me my current glucose reading. I was taking measurements approximately six times per day that informed me of my current sugar level (low, normal or high). Not so bad, but also not good enough. A person without diabetes is measured constantly by their body and insulin is dispersed as frequently. For me, this manual process resulted in only a fraction of the knowledge I needed to accurately manage myself (and I was not able to measure my sugars while asleep). For the first few years, my sugar levels were volatile at best. A non-diabetic person's glucose profile looks very stable from day to day (almost a straight line), while mine looked more like a roller-coaster. I was either frequently very low (which meant not enough energy to function or live—your brain uses 20% of all your glucose needs), or I was very high (which meant the high glucose in my body was destroying my vascular and nervous systems). Either way, high or low, you don't feel so well when always on a roller-coaster, and you don't feel normal. So, the objective for me was to make my sugar levels more stable, more normal.

I started a journey to see how I could better manage my diabetes. At first, it seemed that I might consider an insulin pump that automatically fed me insulin hourly, which ideally would help me maintain a more normal glucose level. At the time there were choices, but few. To date, over the last 10 years, I have used four different insulin pumps and two different continuous glucose meters. Two of the four insulin pumps nearly killed me. My first pump was a mechanical wearable patch pump which distributed insulin at a consistent rate (basal rate). It turns out that it was geared to provide insulin at a higher basal rate than I needed, so it quickly caused low blood sugars. I had to tear the pump off shortly after installing it. The second pump was a very nice product, but was also geared toward people who needed more insulin than I needed on a daily basis. While it did not nearly kill me, it was a nuisance to use as it was constantly sounding an alarm, interrupting my quality of life. And neither of the continuous glucose monitors interoperated with the first three insulin pumps. It was my third pump that put me in the hospital again for a condition called diabetic ketoacidosis (DKA), a condition where your blood sugars are so high that only an ICU visit can reverse it (I nearly died because of a failure with an insulin pump). I later learned that the pump's canula (which distributes the insulin) failed, so it was time to move on. In my mind, they were more experiments. Not fully mechanically or electronically proven.

Today I'm on a new system, one where my insulin pump actually talks/interoperates with my continuous glucose monitor while predicting my insulin needs much more frequently and more accurately than any other device or system I've used before (I use the Tandem T:Slim X2 insulin pump, which interoperates with the Dexcom G6 continuous glucose monitor; the combination of these devices is FDA-approved[1]). While this insulin pump can fail, at least it's connected to a continuous monitoring system that can alert me that it has failed. I feel much better; I sleep much better; I love what technology and wearable technology have done for me. This is the future.

Technology can help us all, chronic or not. We need to embrace it, innovate it and create and invent like never before. Innovation on top of invention and future innovation on top of this means that tomorrow, there will be many more options for all of us. The difference between today and tomorrow is that wearable sensors will certainly play a major role in enabling all of us to scientifically manage and monitor our conditions; and not just diseases, but also proactively and continuously manage our health, physical and mental awareness and performance. This is already witnessed today with technology and as described within this book, via wearable sensor devices utilizing the assistance of predictive algorithms, situational awareness systems, artificial intelligence, machine learning and engagement practices.

More importantly, the ability to monitor your vital signs yourself in near-real-time and continuously means that you have the control, the ability to learn the behaviors that may affect your chronic condition, your proactive health, and your physical and mental performance. What I learned with wearable and continuous monitoring was the specific foods that affected my high or low blood sugars the most. I changed my diet so I could achieve more normal blood sugar levels. I learned the precise difference between choosing between highly processed foods and whole foods, between fast foods and a great salad, between foods that contain either high or low carbs. I also learned the effect of exercise and the effect a long-distance run or workout would have on my insulin needs, and how quickly my blood sugar would drop while exercising. We all could benefit from knowing the near-immediate effects of the mental and physical choices we make.

To me, wearable technology seems to be more about the extension of our awareness beyond what we can sense ourselves. The technology exists today to monitor many of our vitals, and through further invention and innovation, there's no doubt in my mind that it can monitor and manage most chronic illnesses and our physical and mental health.

## Note

1  https://investor.tandemdiabetes.com/news-releases/news-release-details/
   tandem-diabetes-care-announces-fda-clearance-tslim-x2-insulin
   also www.healthline.com/diabetesmine/new-diabetes-technology-
   expected-2019#Diabetes-Products-to-Watch-for-in-2019

# Chapter 2

# The Adoption of Wearables

Chris Landon MD, FAAP, FCCP, FRSM

## Contents

I have been involved in remote patient monitoring for over fifty years. The advent of the smartphone as opposed to a two-kilobyte per second little straw to try and suck an elephant's worth of data represents a significant advancement for effectively using remote patient monitoring data. The smartphone has provided a platform, making remote patient monitoring finally accessible for effective patient management. The advent of COVID-19 has provided something that the CMS remote patient monitoring billing codes did not, and that is a real life-or-death use case.

Remote patient monitoring has been one of the fastest-growing healthcare trends for improving post-acute care and reducing hospital readmissions in pilot after pilot. But widespread implementation has been a harder sell. The new opportunity for reimbursement from the Centers for Medicare and Medicaid Services (CMS) is applied only to the Medicare population, which may be technology-averse, and to doctors who share those feelings. Health insurers now have Innovation Centers to evaluate remote monitoring, blockchain, AI and its effect on population health, cost reductions, and as a marketing tool to employers.

When I participate in programs such as Health Achieve in Toronto, I am bombarded by physicians who applaud the home blood pressure monitoring, but do not want to review and take responsibility for the results. Choosing a low-risk high-reward disease state, co-operative reimbursed physicians, and the right technology partners has greatly improved wearables adoption. Implementation has become fairly simple and mostly managed by vendors, with minimal effort from your IT staff. There does remain concern among the IT staff that the EHR may not have FHIR access for your solution, as well as the current provision of an access point from ransomware.

As an organization, a successful remote patient monitoring launch requires consideration of clinical, financial, and operational impacts and planning, which cannot come from just one of those aspects. Which patient populations will benefit the most? Who owns the hardware? What is the best form factor? Which vendors? How good is the security of the devices? Are costs controlled and is there clinical, financial, and operational benefit?

The marriage of clinical experience and technology can be a good one, but is fraught with peril. Often self-funded, a physician will dedicate considerable time and resources programming a solution to the narrow problem that he or she faces in the Emergency Room or office, and end up unable to overcome the pragmatic, territorial, and at times seemingly diabolic denial of entry into the electronic health record. The business of technology is the third ingredient requiring key partners, key activities, key resources, value propositions, customer relationships, channels, customer segments, cost structure, and revenue streams. The noble digital futurist must become the digital realist.

With the advent of COVID-19, the digital realist has finally moved from the eternal hell of "early adopters" to the need for contact-less visits, reduced admissions and readmissions, actual adoption of form factors, CMS reimbursement for Medicare patient remote patient care moving into the private insurance arena, improved ease of use of video teleconferencing, and patient readiness with access to technology. In keeping with our clinical, financial, operational theme—physicians receive CMS reimbursement for dispensing and demonstrating the use of the device under Medicare remote patient management codes, as well as monthly reimbursement for the dispensed device.

The old days of bringing a bottle of whiskey to the head of Purchasing have been replaced by a simple formula. What is the cost, beyond just the device, and what is the return on the investment, both initially and ongoing?

## Which Patient Populations Would Benefit Most?

Trying to keep a coherent multi-disciplinary mission and team must start with the patient. Geography, access to specialists, and expensive disease states that require monitoring are the factors that drove the original commitment by the United States Department of Agriculture Distance Learning and Telemedicine grants. Keeping farmers in their communities with access to "big city" orthopedists, cardiologists, diabetologists, and so forth meant a commitment at both ends of the digital pipe through ISDN lines and a commitment to education and availability by the primary care practitioner and specialist. We have participated in the process for over three decades and watched equipment improve while other system components decline. Challenges include champion physicians who rapidly turned over in the public health system, front office staff unaccustomed to scheduling who commit valuable clinic rooms for an hour that could turn over four patients in the same amount of time, and poorly functioning broadband or cellular connectivity. To compensate, physicians had to rely on phone and fax machines to improve care and outcomes.

For monitoring congestive heart failure, we would take serial pictures of the patient's foot in a shoe box, trans-telephonic monitoring of peak flow in asthma, home blood pressure cuffs with phone follow-up. There must be a willingness of the healthcare practitioner to review the results of all those wearable blood pressure results. Is there a clinical impact? Does care change? Does the doctor review all the results with all the patients? When does he do that? Is he able to be paid for this time? Clinical, financial, and operational may be very specific to wearable continuous glucose monitor hour representation, even splitting it into four-hour segments for fine-tuning. Now we have a window into patients' lives. Will the patient population want this invasion of their personal space?

Wearables and remote monitoring systems that attach to the computer in your pocket changed that. Now our use cases can include moving postsurgical care to the home. We have worked with 11Health, whose inspiring patient founder passed away too soon, in developing a "smart colostomy bag". What became clear over time is that the first thirty days of continuous monitoring and alerts prevented readmission for dehydration, the integrative healthcare coordinators provided needed support, but if the colostomy bag itself leaked, despite all the impressive sensors and dashboards, it needed to return for more development.

Choosing a vendor must reflect the patient's doctor needs and the patient's willingness to have their healthcare improved through integrating this device into their lives. The vendor solution should be expandable to other chronic diseases, and it should have a high yield of clinically relevant information.

## Technology and Design Considerations

Bring Your Own Device has been the mantra with downloadable apps and ability to enter information and receive notifications. Managing and supporting these solutions has proven problematic with a lack of security, regular changes in iOS and Android updates, maintenance of application software, and security issues.

Bring Your Own Device solutions with apps that need updating with every twist of iOS have led to customized devices. The cost of a customized device has to fit within CMS guidelines, be of high quality, and leave room for potential profit. One device company formerly made toys, and although price-competitive, their devices were prone to breakage.

Preconfigured mobile devices streamline the user experience and allow additional functionality. For example, in the developmental pathway for AgeWell Biometrics, an AI-driven sensor allowing prediction of falls before they occur, and the addition of an emergency button on the sensor in the event of a fall, provide additional needed functionality.

## Ergonomic Considerations

Although many applications have been moved to the wrist, we have found the ring to be well tolerated and reliable. For pulse oximetry not all sensors are created equal, particularly for persons of color. The use of the accelerometer in devices provides good measures of activity level more accurately and reliably than patient surveys, but is also present in the smartphone.

COVID-19 has moved the needle for pulse oximetry and provided additional direction for rings, watches, patches, AI-powered apps, and non-contact vital signs monitoring. The ketogenic diet has accustomed people to measuring their own urine, breath, and blood with well-designed user interfaces.

## Innovative Manufacturer and Vendor Considerations

It is important for your practice or institution to leave room for the "next shiny thing" and support innovative manufacturers. To provide the best solution for the clinical, financial, and operational issues you are addressing takes responsible, knowledgeable understanding of each of those arenas. Does the solution provide the information the healthcare practitioner can use? Is the solution function billable and serviceable within your budget? Will the manufacturer continue to in-service new patients and practitioners?

Emerging and innovative remote patient monitoring solutions are hard to launch. The innovators may be start-up businesses; they are looking to break into their first healthcare organization; they may have focused individual case studies but not have faced large institutional needs; and they may not have references from other systems that have successfully demonstrated the use of their solution. Individual patient monitoring versus large populations is approached differently. Their solution must be able to scale up and down by patient load and pricing.

The Electronic Health Record (EHR) vendors, from a start-up perspective, have provided foreboding barriers to integration. The declaration that a remote patient monitoring solution can be integrated based on current standards is much different than if EHR integration has been accomplished and is live.

In these days of increasing institution ransomware and hacking of personal health information, questions regarding cyber security, data breaches, response to data breaches, and HIPAA compliance are a mandatory requirement.

Additionally, customer support and service from the vendor are needed for patients, healthcare workers, and IT. Essential customer support questions should be asked of other institutions that have implemented the solutions, as well as the vendors.

## Evaluating the Physician Experience

The physician experience has to be considered in its entirety. We had received a grant from the USDA Rural Development plan to provide remote islands with a telemedicine solution for multiple island clinics. We choose a vendor with a clinic in a bag—electronic stethoscope, ultrasound, general exam camera, dermatoscope, and so forth in a manageable bag with a patient care record that, with internet connectivity, not only recorded the data for consultation, recurring visits, but also a cloud-based interpretation. Unexpected factors were the loss of their fiber optic cable leading to 3G connectivity at best, making personal communication difficult in onboarding, the closing of several of the clinics, and the recent adoption of an electronic healthcare record. The electronic health record was affordable but difficult to institute, and the need to double-enter patient info led to a rejection of the solution.

How the physicians receive, review, and implement data should not be ignored. I will never forget being cornered by very polite Canadians at a health show for reviewing a vendor providing remote blood pressure monitoring. Evidently reviewing up to hundreds of blood pressure readings every Monday, to be reviewed with responsibility but not compensation, was not looked upon with favor. Working with the vendor on screening abnormal values, patients with medication changes within the last thirty days, and so forth brought those numbers to operational and clinical usability.

## Patient Considerations

The last inch logistics of getting the device to the patient, making a complete solution, educating the patient and practitioner, and integrating with IT are essential questions to answer. IT departments are essential to the process of patient engagement and satisfaction, and relish their role and control as the quarterbacks. Nerds no more: without them, you are doomed to failure.

## The Healthcare Cost Focus

The final criteria revolve around the control of costs. Choosing your partner requires seamless integration, service, and connectivity. The bundling of product and connectivity has helped to bring down the overall cost of some solutions.

The goal is to improve patient outcomes (clinical), have an integrated solution (operational), and save the healthcare organization money or provide profit to the physician (e.g., financial). A proper relationship in which the vendor has thought through and solved the problems, interacts cordially with IT, on-boards healthcare workers, and educates and supports patients will lead to the best part: improving healthcare and the experience of healthcare for patients and professionals.

## Internet of Wearables

IoT continues to unite us all with technology in ways previously unimaginable. Advances with IoT connectivity for 2020 is happening for nearly every industry, including healthcare. Healthcare adoption outside of a doctor's or provider's clinical environment has been slow to develop due to the challenge of achieving key regulatory, policy, technology, and interoperability hurdles necessary for its acceptance worldwide. However, in the epoch of COVID-19, this will change, expanding much more quickly due to the vision of IoT thought leaders in remote monitoring healthcare whose sole focus has been on data interoperability.

Leading this IoT movement for tele-health, tele-medicine and tele-monitoring is the IEEE Personal Health Devices Working Group, which works benevolently and collaboratively with health, technology, life sciences, public policy, research, and advocacy groups worldwide to make possible the necessary social change, personal health engagement, positive behavior change, digital therapeutics, healthy longevity, and improved wellbeing and health outcomes. The IEEE PHD WG is passionately focused on driving this agenda, creating the evidence base and mobilizing collective action to achieve personal connected health all throughout a person's lifespan. The latest example of the IEEE PHD WG's success and leadership is with their alignment with the Continua Design Guidelines (CDG) and Health Level 7 (HL7) Fast Healthcare Interoperability Resources (FHIR).

The IEEE PHD WG is responsible for convening the global technology industry standards and thought leaders to develop medical-grade and end-to-end, plug-and-play IoT connectivity for connected health. They have been the pioneers in establishing standards-based guidelines and security for connected health technologies such as sensors, remote monitoring devices, tablets, wearables, watches, gateways, and smartphones, as well as networked and cloud solutions. Today, the CDG has completed all disease states initially envisioned for remote monitoring in 2006. These include diabetes, heart failure, hypertension, COPD, health, wellness, and fitness protocols and guidelines. This represents twenty-six data protocols from forty health, medical, and fitness device capabilities, enabling hundreds of different product types that can now be certified to the CDG today—and all with a direct path to the EHR.

## COVID-19 Wellness Monitoring Turns to Health Monitoring

I became involved in the evolution of personal vital sign monitoring in the 1990s with Vivometrics. With a gorgeous vest with Lifeshirt written vertically across the zipper, we integrated heart rate, respiratory rate with respiratory inductive plethysmography, blood pressure, pulse oximetry, and other measures DARPA won't let me mention. With algorithms derived from my asthma, COPD, and cystic fibrosis patients, we home-monitored and interpreted sleep patterns for first responders, race car drivers, astronauts, and athletes. At fifteen thousand dollars per Lifeshirt, our business model depended on big Pharma research, grants, and CMS recognizing home sleep studies at a rate that matched the costs. Unfortunately, the 2008 economic meltdown took out the funds that it took to stay at that expensive cutting edge. CMS didn't recognize home sleep studies until it met their economic model. The software was recreated and is now used in the study of early intervention for neuromuscular diseases, and the cost of the form factor has dropped to ten percent of what it was.

Extraordinary developments allowed the long-anticipated breakout moment for remote patient monitoring. CMS has provided billing codes for Medicare that allow the dispensing of the device, human counseling based on the results, and a long-term proposition of clinic investment in devices with payback through continued use.

In dealing constantly with wearable startups, I see many unique ideas that have received sweat equity, friends, fools and family financing, and very clever and triumphant code writers with software in the Apple store brought to their knees by the constant changing of the Apple iOS or Android not being available or not working among the family of devices.

That all started to change last year when the Centers for Medicare and Medicare Services (CMS) changed its reimbursement rules to make RPM more accessible. Then COVID-19 came along and made it essential. There will be a retreat from telehealth payment by insurers as the pandemic slows down.

Sheltering in place has revealed the need for seniors and patients with chronic diseases needing more frequent and convenient visits to monitor lab and remote patient monitoring tools, without being exposed to influenza, RSV, rhinovirus, and other transmissible respiratory diseases. Remote patient monitoring allows even patients who are non-critical COVID-positive to continue being monitored at home. Even in my clinic, I am only getting a two-minute snapshot. Augmenting the telehealth visit with digital scale, oximetry, blood pressure, heart rate, respiratory rate, sleep study, and exercise capability allows a ten-thousand-foot view, and with the addition of machine learning, the ability to predict exacerbations.

Beyond reducing admissions and allowing earlier discharge, the true goal is preventing readmissions. Improving patient outcomes requires improved compliance rates and patients taking ownership of their own healthcare. This provides a different target from wellness, moving it to health with measurable consequences of remote patient monitoring. The Chronic Care Management Program of CMS has been predicated on these assumptions and in targeted high utility has shown benefit.[1]

COVID-19 has only underlined the direction CMS has taken from only reimbursing remote monitoring in rural or remote areas to the 2018 99091 reimbursement code. We have participated in the predecessor program through the United States Department of Agriculture Rural Utilities Service Distance Learning and Telemedicine Program, aimed at keeping farmers in their hometowns. The cost of equipment and expansion of bandwidth were supported, but with a target of physician champions who left after two years of service, it has been a difficult journey. The unfounded comprehensive grant writing and project administration, project funds advanced by the applying organization, and the lack of support for actual physician consultation services has made it a difficult program for us to continue to be part of. The new CMS reimbursement rules, extended to include chronic disease or coronavirus, have been extended by some private insurers as well.

Beyond usable and actionable data, the key has been improved ease of use. Heart rate, movement, and sleep patterns are built into wearables through form factors such as the watch; Bluetooth-connected blood pressure cuffs, blood glucose monitors, and weight scales upload data through smartphones and tablets. What to do with all this information has encountered two hurdles. Information overload for the physicians was clearly demonstrated to me when I was approached, politely, by Canadian physicians at a conference. They asked me what I wanted them to do with three hundred

---

[1] https://mathematica.org/publications/evaluation-of-the-diffusion-and-impact-of-the-chronic-care-management-ccm-services-final-report

blood pressure records every Monday, which they were supposed to review if they accepted them and were responsible for any missed pathology. This led to better guidelines and clinically intuitive screens based on patient goals of reduced systolic hypertension, new medication changes which, in the face of "white coat hypertension," might lead to hypotension at home.

The failure of electronic healthcare records to accept the data directly, leading to scanned-in PDF documents, is now being more directly addressed by the CURES Act.

The mandate, a rare piece of bipartisan legislation, was signed into law in 2016 to increase choices and access for patients and providers, to streamline development and delivery for drugs and medical devices, accelerate research into serious illnesses, address the opioid crisis, and improve mental health services. A balance between decreasing regulatory burdens associated with the EHR and health information technology and advancing interoperability concentrated on a key sales strategy used by the EHR vendors—lack of interoperability. Information blocking by preventing and interfering with access to health information, exchange of health information, and input of information from devices forced institutions to choose an EHR with a silo. By April 15, 2021, it finally took effect, having passed through the ONC, CMS, and HHS. When a patient asks for their data elements, there are mandated options available:

- Printing the data from the EHR
- Exporting it through a Continuity of Care Document (CCD) in the EHR
- Directing patients to view and download data using a patient portal

This includes the data elements seen here. www.healthit.gov/isa/united-states-core-data-interoperability-uscdi#uscdi-v1

The so-called ONC Final Rule, beyond data sharing, puts pressure on remote health monitoring wearables to support Application Program Interface (API) functionality and to certify the health IT through the ONC Health IT Certification Program to bring about standardization. The development of this API token/electronic key makes it possible for software applications to connect. This alone did not solve the problem, as there isn't a consistent way to plug an API token into an app such as Apple Health. The goal of the CURES Act, to allow a new market of health apps to leverage data from any electronic healthcare record in a single standard non-proprietary format, is underway through Fast Healthcare Interoperability Resources (FHIR).

# Chapter 3

# The Future of Wearables

Laurie M. Orlov

## Contents

## Wearables Can Change the Lives of Older Adults

### *The Wearables Adoption Trend Is Driven by Fitness, Health*

**Wearables are nothing new—except in how they are used.** The Quantified Self movement, coined as a term by two *Wired Magazine* writers

DOI: 10.4324/9781003304036-4

in 2007, simply described the growing interest in tracking those personal characteristics that could be useful in managing health and wellbeing. From activity trackers that gained popularity in the past decade, to the introduction of smartwatches by Apple in 2015, interest has exploded and capabilities have blossomed.

**Forecasts of purchases are rising.** eMarketer forecasts the numbers of adult users out to 2024 (see Figure 3.1), and IDC forecasts growth in shipments of wearables out to 2024 (see Figure 3.2). According to one Apple Watch insider, at least 3–5 million Apple watches have been purchased by adults age 65+. Gartner's January 2021 forecast of $81.5 billion in growth was driven by increased consumer interest in tracking health status during the pandemic (on smartwatches) and the growth of remote work (purchases and upgrades to headphones and ear-worn devices).

**Views on the patient's role in their own medical care have changed.** In 2013, Leroy Hood published a paper, "Systems Biology and P4 Medicine: Past, Present, and Future," which introduced the idea that patients had a role in their own care, saying that medicine should be "predictive, preventive, personalized, and participatory." That concept helps explain the growing interest in wearables, as they are capable of assisting in all four

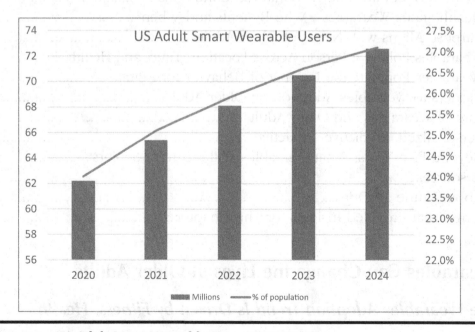

**Figure 3.1 US Adult Smart Wearable Users 2020–2024**
*Source:* **eMarketer.**

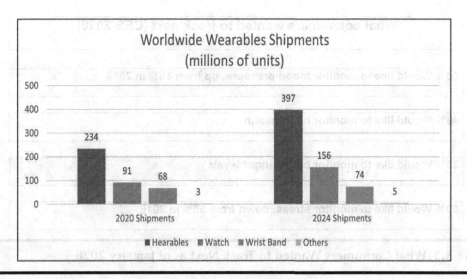

**Figure 3.2    IDC Shipment Forecast of Wearables in Units to 2024.**

attributes. And researchers are seeking new ways to use wearables to detect problems that may be unnoticed, like an impending stroke.

*"Most people having a stroke do not recognize when it is happening and ignore the changes as unimportant. Our goal is to detect symptoms and alert."* Sandra Saldana, **Alva Health**

**Guidance is emerging suggesting what may be important to track.** Even before the Covid-19 pandemic, as of January 2020, the Guidance for Wearable Health Solutions white paper noted that users of wearables are beginning to show preferences about what to track, specifically about tracking changes in blood pressure and other aspects of heart health.

> As physicians we represent 15% of the positive outcome. The rest is genetics and behavior change. To impact outcomes, that will only happen if we know who a person is. I predict that these wearables will become a walking medical device over time—and will change the practice of medicine.
>
> —Dr. Hon Pak, Chief Medical Officer, **Samsung Electronics**

**Consumers have begun to indicate their preferences.** Because individuals want to participate in their own health, they not only want to track, but also to share data with their doctor to help with a more accurate diagnosis. The Consumer Technology Association has been surveying consumers, noting that even in February 2019, 58% of consumers were

| What consumers wanted to track next (CES 2020) |
|---|
| 55% Would like to monitor blood pressure, up from 46% in 2016 |
| 49% Would like to monitor heart health |
| 33% Would like to monitor blood sugar levels |
| 50% Would like to monitor stress, down from 55% in 2016 |

**Figure 3.3  What Consumers Wanted to Track Next as of January 2020.**

willing to share health data with their doctor to gain a more accurate diagnosis and more effective treatment. But wearable innovations are appearing daily—and can still outpace the ability of physicians to keep up. At 2020's CES event, responders identified specific areas of interest (see Figure 3.3).

**Health-tracking devices and usage grew in 2020**. According to Rock Health, 66% of those who started using a wearable did so to manage a diagnosed health condition. And more than 51% of wearables owners use the device to manage a diagnosed health condition. Specific health attributes included weight, heart rate, and blood pressure. It should be noted data was collected prior to the 2020 Covid-19 lockdowns (See Figure 3.4).

> Physicians can drive adoption, but they have their day jobs—how do they know what works and what doesn't? Given the pace of technological change, we should be looking seriously at more comprehensive development of industry standards and perhaps accreditation for health technology to help properly guide clinicians.
> —Rene Quashie, VP, Policy and Regulatory Affairs, Digital Health, **Consumer Technology Association**

> Wearables help establish a personalized baseline by getting validated signals as an early warning to seek other testing—such as cognition, hypertension, arrythmia, or atrial fibrillation.
> —Ryan Kraudel, VP Marketing, **Valencell**

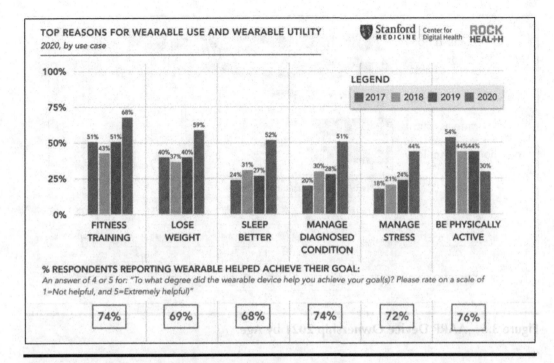

**Figure 3.4  Reasons for Wearable Health Use.**

*Source:* Stanford, Rock Health

## What about Older Adults and Their Usage of Wearables?

In 2019, HIMSS published a literature review about wearable technologies in medicine, observing from its research that medical-grade wearables had potential, but that it might be difficult to get seniors to wear them, perhaps due to lack of awareness. But just two years later, attitudes have changed. The smartwatch was legitimized as an alternative to the Personal Emergency Response Service (PERS) pendant on the day that Apple announced fall detection in 2018. In fact, Apple dominates the smartwatch category, though Samsung and Fitbit are competitive and also being recommended for seniors. And AARP's newest technology adoption report notes that 20% of the 70+ age range own a wearable. Also notable, considering that most wearables are still paired with them, is that smartphone ownership has risen most sharply among the 70+, with 77% of survey responders indicating they own one (See Figure 3.5).

**Now women AND men are acquiring Apple watches.** Initially it was a "guy thing"—an Apple Watch was perceived to make one look cool. While Apple product purchases in 2015 were largely made by older men, by 2019,

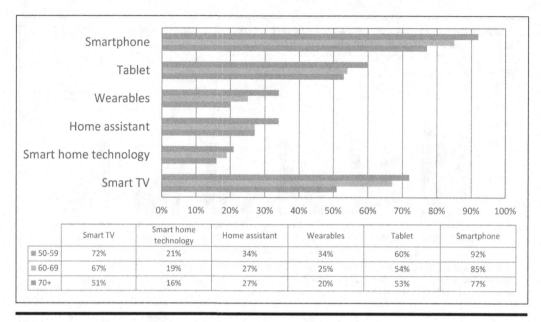

| | Smart TV | Smart home technology | Home assistant | Wearables | Tablet | Smartphone |
|---|---|---|---|---|---|---|
| ■ 50-59 | 72% | 21% | 34% | 34% | 60% | 92% |
| ■ 60-69 | 67% | 19% | 27% | 25% | 54% | 85% |
| ■ 70+ | 51% | 16% | 27% | 20% | 53% | 77% |

**Figure 3.5   AARP Device Ownership 2021 by Age.**

women liked them too—and nearly half of the watches are purchased by women. Though the absolute percentage is still low, older adults represented greatest growth, up 15% in 2019.

**Gaining control of your own aging.** The Apple Watch was also a pioneer in offering health-related information. Today, health advice or guides are available on other products, like watches that can take blood pressure readings correlated with a cuff. And with some devices today, correlation is unnecessary. Wearables with actionable health information will increasingly appeal to the 80% of older adults who have at least one chronic condition (See Figure 3.6).

> "A person used to walk 5 miles and now walks only one. Regardless
> of frailty level—people want to be in control of their own aging."
> —Jean Anne Booth, Founder, **UnaliWear**

## What Trends Made Wearables for Older Adults Viable Now?

Not long ago, it would have been impossible to imagine the growing use of wearables overall, let alone by older adults. Specific market trends converged to enable the change, as:

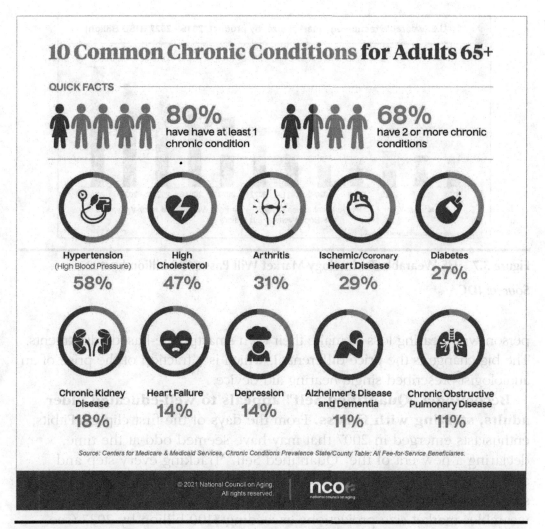

**Figure 3.6  Ten Common Chronic Conditions for Adults Aged 65+.**
*Source:* NCOA.

**Self-service hearables have made hearing improvements cool—and cheap.** Just as the smartwatch disrupted the medical alert world, so too have hearables jostled the world of hearing aids. The amplification technology inside earbuds and Bluetooth headsets is much like that inside audiologist-fitted hearing aids. Firms like Nuheara and Bose have produced self-fitting hearables that are FDA-approved and can be bought online. And the overt style of ear-worn devices is popularizing hearables across a broad spectrum of users—Apple sold 100 million AirPods in 2020. And Alango combines a hearable with self-service or retail hearing tests to enable a

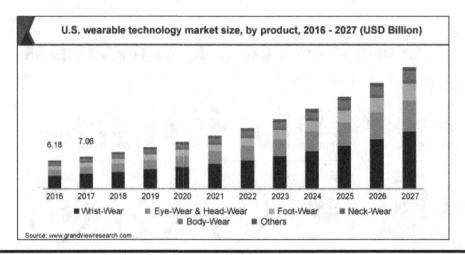

**Figure 3.7    US Wearable Technology Market Will Pass $100 billion by 2027.**
*Source:* IDC.

person with hearing loss to make their own smartphone-based adjustments. The big change is the price differential, which is a fraction of the price of an audiologist-prescribed single hearing aid device.

**Becoming a "Quantified Self" appeals to well-educated older adults, starting with fitness.** From the days of the first clip-on Fitbits, enthusiasts emerged in 2007 that may have seemed odd at the time, declaring a new era of the "Quantified Self." Tracking every step and activity from the first "I got up at 6:20 this morning" to measuring mood, sleep, heart rate, food, exercise has become mainstream by 2021—with wearables market size projections exceeding $100 billion by 2027 (see Figure 3.7). Device makers like Apple and Samsung saw the trend and seized on it to galvanize business in the face of slowing phone sales— Apple alone had sold 43 million smartwatches by the end of 2020 (See Figure 3.7).

**Seniors want to look cool—the Apple Watch made cool PERS wearables possible.** This one device galvanized a stagnant industry that was stuck in a 30-year cycle of selling bulky medical alert pendants to 82-year-old women living alone. Within a year or two of Apple Watch launching, PERS vendors began offering personal emergency response services in a wrist-worn and unobtrusive wearable. These smartwatches eliminated the stigma of wearing a pendant that declares "You're Old." And app makers like Fall Call Solutions and Best Buy crafted apps to run on the watch that offer the fall detection service connected to a needed 24x7 response center.

**Senior living tech interest grows—Smartwatches may replace pendants there, too.** In the post-Covid era, some senior living companies are promoting technology for residents, and some are touting the benefits of wearables. Those with fall detection, RPM, and a 24x7 notification process are being described by senior-focused websites as useful to older adults and caregivers.

> We are on a journey into Remote Patient Monitoring (RPM) in senior-living—co-developing a watch with Harvard. This is funded through a Covid grant.
>
> —Nick Patel, CEO, **ThriveWell**

## Wearables Monitor Poorly Monitored Conditions

Given the preponderance of chronic conditions among the 65+ population, the opportunity to detect, intervening at the right time, may be one of the most significant digital health advances in recent years. As studies confirm accuracy and benefit, their role in healthcare will grow because:

**Wearables can augment and potentially inform the annual checkup.** Instead of the one-time annual blood pressure check, perhaps elevated in the presence of a nurse, monitoring blood pressure at home provides a level of accuracy that could help avoid over-medicating. Instead of periodic finger sticks to determine blood sugar levels, a blood sugar patch can indicate both the impact of certain foods and provide a timely warning.

> Wearables can provide a longitudinal view of the patient's health. At the doctor's office, weight and height are useless—what were they in between visits, what were sleep patterns? The problems between intervening visits could be solved.
>
> —Rene Quashie, VP, **CTA**

**Wearables can be useful for specific diseases and health issues.** Research is underway about the role of wearables to trigger a conversation with a healthcare team about medication dosage or timing for Parkinson's patients whose activity level has changed. Or using a wrist-worn wearable, perhaps a provider could be able to detect a sudden change in body temperature, spiking blood pressure or the onset of a stroke—seeing events that are otherwise unnoticed.

> Digital therapeutics and wearables could be very useful for monitoring the health of patients. There is an opportunity for a middleware provider of software that uses AI to assess whether a particular issue is important or not to alert a health care provider or call 911 for a medical emergency.
>
> —Rick Robinson (Innovation),
> Michael Phillips (Technology Strategy), **AARP**

## Health-Status Wearables—Who Benefits and When?

Advances in wearable technology, vendor excitement, and growing consumer adoption might lead one to think that the integration into healthcare processes is a given. But while some leaders are excited by possibilities, other health professionals express doubt about near-term data integration of consumer wearable data. Yet clearly researchers and investors don't believe it—innovation is accelerating, and huge streams of money pour into new companies as:

**Miniaturization now enables multi-function wearables.** The same device can track your steps, tell you to stand up, detect if you have an irregular heart rate, and take your blood pressure. And that is just the minimum capability of devices and software today. When data from these devices is transmitted to end-user health profiles, insights and predictions about future change will become mainstream. And when it is aggregated with other data sets, expect further insights about population health. In the meantime, these multi-function and relatively tiny devices—with their alerts, nudges, and trend reports—represent possibilities just for the Apple Watch alone that six years ago could not be imagined. But as with other tech changes, skyrocketing adoption of one vendor's offering has created a market opportunity for many others.

**Research is pouring into new uses—spinning out ideas and companies.** Researchers today are looking at the possibility of wearables being used to predict strokes (based on motion changes) before they occur—or to guide a Parkinson's patient to get a new prescription (based on gait changes). In early 2021, Boston University selected Shimmer wearables for a brain-heart health study; Scripps Research launched a study about wearables and precision medicine; and Penn State is studying the medical application of wearable antennas.

**Investments into wearable health offerings are staggering . . .** Investors see a New Era for Virtual Health that includes both in-home technology and wearables. The Series C announcement for the Ōura Ring is a case in point—$100 million of investment as of May 2021, with multiple research initiatives underway in the context of chronic and acute diseases. As founder Harpreet Singh Rai noted, the wearables market is now measured in trillions of dollars worldwide. Hinge Health just raised $300 million for its health-coaching offering that has a wearable sensor, and Kaiser Permanente and Mayo Clinic just put $100 million into Medically Home. In 2020, health measurement startup Whoop raised $100 million.

. . . **All this is despite assertions that doctors don't need or want the data.** Because consumer interest is growing, surveyed doctors today use and/or recommend wearables. But according to a 2020 survey by Deloitte, while interest in wearables has increased, the actual integration of data from patient wearables has grown little in the past two years—from 5% to 10% of surveyed physicians. And Forrester's survey of 40 physicians and patients concluded that wearables today are for consumers, not physicians—asserting that "doctors don't need the data." But that may change if worried well consumers walk into the office with higher-quality blood pressure data than the physician can obtain during intermittent visits.

## Purpose Aligns with Needs of Older Adults

Wearable devices and what they can track may be the key to the much-repeated concepts of aging well or successful aging. While the measurements that wearables yield may be fun and motivating for the young, their purpose closely aligns with the needs of an aging population—especially 10,000 Baby Boomers turning 65 each day. Either older adults already see these benefits or those who care for and about them will. As wearables improve in quality and accuracy over time, they will enable asking questions that invite longitudinal understanding and proactive interventions—for example:

**How fit are we over time?** Is activity, mobility, energy improving, remaining the same, or declining? One interviewee noted after recovery from Covid how proud he is to "close all the measurement rings on the Apple Watch 108 days in a row" and if one isn't closed, he will get up, go out, and take another walk.

> My wearable can pick up data from my bike, putting heartrate or general fitness status on my watch. It keeps me healthy and paying attention to that information.
>
> —Rob Flippo, CEO **MobileHelp**

**How is our health in the context of chronic conditions?** Are measurements of body signals showing that all is well? When tracking metrics ourselves—such as blood pressure, blood sugar, heart rhythm, heartrate variability, heart rate recovery after exercise—is everything okay? For those at risk of stroke recurrence—is there a way to know in advance and get the right treatment?

> I am interested in resting heart rate—I had Covid in October, so I began using more measurements. Today I am lifting heavier weights and my recovery time is down from five minutes to one minute.
> —Paul Barter, Managing Partner, **Paul Barter & Associates**

**What is happening to those we care about?** Will wearable remote patient monitoring technologies help them recover after illness and avoid repeat hospitalizations that result from mismanaged medications? Will the data from wearables help a family member know whether an older adult is adhering to physician regimens following hospital discharge?

> We are rapidly approaching a point where aspects of "hospital-at-home" will become viable with a combination of wearables, robotics and passive sensors. At a post-clinical level, these tools will provide actionable data that support post-acute recovery, communicate changes in condition and influence behaviors which would improve health management over time.
> —Michael Skaff, COO, **Jewish Senior Living Group**

## *Wearables Follow a Person Across Location, Time, and Health*

Despite the presumed low probability of integrating data from wearables directly into the health system, their utility may make a significant difference in wellbeing for an older individual. Unlike a computer, smartphone, or camera, wearables (such as a Bluetooth headset, a smart wristband or ring, smart jewelry, or glasses) are worn on the body. They can assist even when an older adult doesn't ask, as with fall detection, whereabouts, or heart issues.

> We are selling a smartwatch with a heart rate monitor, a pedometer and immediate contact with a monitored call center. One customer family bought it for their Mom who likes to garden in the yard.
> —*Kelly Johnson, Co-Founder and COO,* ***Hands-Free Health***

**What types of wearable devices offer potential for older adults?**
Depending on their health status (or chronic conditions), devices listed can
be useful, engaging, informative, lifesaving, or predictive. Given options in
each category, the guides listed in the Resources section at the end of this
report may also be worth a look. For specific wellness categories, there are
also websites specific to that condition (or device) that can offer more guidance. In addition, experts expect that more FDA-described Combination
Devices will emerge over time that track several metrics, noting that today
it's still an early market. Category examples include (see Figure 3.8):

**Smartwatches with health features.** For Apple Watch owners, it
takes a bit of work to get the device to stop making suggestions or change

| Category | What it is | Examples |
|---|---|---|
| Hearables/earbuds | An amplification ear-worn wearable | Apple AirPods, WearandHear, Dime |
| Smartwatches | Smart watches monitoring activity, health metrics | Apple, Samsung, Fitbit, Garmin, Adapt |
| Headsets – AR/VR | Internet-connected glasses enable alternate views | MyndVR, Embodied Labs, Rendever |
| Fitness trackers (no watch) | Step counter, heart rate | Amazon Halo, Vivo, Whoop Strap 3, Fitbit One |
| Continuous diabetes wearables | Scans detect blood sugar level, patch injects insulin | FreeStyle Libre, Dexcom G5, |
| Sleep trackers | Wearables noted for sleep tracking | Ōura Ring, Whoop, Fitbit Versa |
| Wrist-worn Health | Low-sleep indicates risk of dementia | Omron HeartGuide, Amazon Halo, Whoop |
| Smart jewelry | Ring, Necklace | Trelaware, ADT invisiWear |
| Dementia zone trackers | Set a range – track movement outside range | MindMe Locate, PocketFinder |
| Medical Grade wearable, data collection | Blood pressure, mobile EKG, Diabetes patch | Omron HeartGuide, AliveCor, Tidepool |
| Medical Alert/PERS/Safety | Emergency call, fall detection – in home or out | Medical Guardian, Lively Wearable, UnaliWear |

Figure 3.8   Examples of Wearable Categories and Some of the Offerings.

the advice—"*I think you are taking an outdoor walk!*" But like other smart-watches, the feedback about steps and patterns, is useful—even addictive. "*You walked more last month than this month!*" New research is underway to develop wearables to assist patients with Parkinson's notice the signs of movement and behavioral issues.

> We are working with people with Parkinson's. Our technology can facilitate a meaningful interaction between the wearer and care teams. The wearable can offer an understanding if a new medication is working or not.
> —Nicholas Constant, **EchoWear LLC**

**Hearables.** A small number of people, relative to the numbers with hearing loss, are helped by hearing aids. According to the World Health Organization, 430 million people worldwide have disabling hearing loss and do not use **ANY** hearing solution to mitigate it. Aside from a sizable price differential, hearables could, according to experts, provide them with some relief:

> Most cases of mild-to-moderately-severe hearing loss can be managed by users themselves, if all the tools work well. The hearing aid advantage will not last more than two years from now.
> —Alexander Goldin, Founder and CEO, **Alango Technologies**

**Diabetes technology.** Continuous Glucose Monitoring (CGM) capabilities have been on the market for years, gradually replacing the 'finger stick' method of checking blood sugar. It requires a prescription today and can be used by the 88 million diabetics (25% of them aged 65+)—even by "quantified selfers" who want to monitor their diet and make adjustments.

**Sleep tracking**. Tracking sleep may be the ultimate aspect of the self to be quantified—the sleep-deprived represent a sizable ($32 billion by 2026) market. Experts agree that sleep (quality or lack) is a significant health indicator—and for older adults, low sleep can heighten risk of dementia.

> We started with sleep. The impact it has, from cognitive function the next day, fasting glucose, hormones, T-cells that fight cancer— these are all linked to our sleep.
> —Harpreet Singh Rai, CEO, **Ōura Ring**

**Fall detection.** Fitness devices prompt older adults to exercise. But one in four of the 65+ population fall each year. Tools like UnaliWear, FallCall Solutions, MobileHelp, or Medical Guardian have technology that can detect a fall and contact a 24/7 response center.

> Apple launched a revolution in the wearable industry and mainstreamed the device. The "smart" fall detection system that we built is a patented API. It can go into any wearable.
>
> —Shea Gregg, CEO, **FallCall Solutions**

## Wearables Populate the Internet of Behavior for Aging

**The Internet of Behavior (IoB) collects data and makes sense of sensing wearables.** In its October 2020 annual conference, Gartner observed a trend—the population of the Internet of Behavior as adjacent and complementary to the Internet of Things. What is it and why is it important for older adults?

> The Internet of Behavior collects the digital dust of people's lives from a variety of sources, and public or private organizations can use this information to influence behavior.
>
> —*Gartner*

Gartner described it as recognition of a phenomenon that already exists, in which everything you do on your smartphone or wearable is tracked

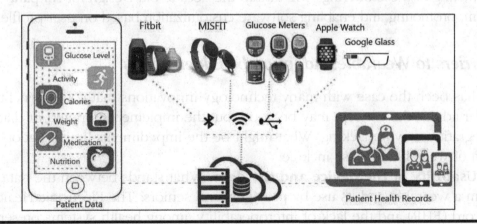

**Figure 3.9   NextGen Healthcare Wearables Will Solidify Today's Tenuous Data Connections.**

*Source:* **https://techno-soft.com/wearable-technology-in-healthcare.html**

and used to show you (or sell you) other items or locations of interest near where you are, what you are looking at, or what you are doing. That is certainly a realistic if somewhat cynical observation. But the Internet of Behavior of aging adults can help manage health, notify caregivers of adverse incidents, or even save their lives.

**IoB will play a role in senior living communities, healthcare settings, and at home.** Of course, there may be negative implications that we already can see from the existing collection of "digital dust." We are startled when an IoB message pops on our phone to tell us something we have looked up only once is sold on the street where we are standing. But consider how an **IoB for Aging** could be remarkably useful. Imagine that Mrs. Smith has not gone near the refrigerator all day and it's 6:00 pm. Tracking movement and motion are already components of senior technology today—but with an Internet of Behavior, patterns in Mrs. Smith's life will be collected and correlated with her other behaviors—like medication adherence, exercise, and social interaction. And these data points could be correlated with fall risk, prompting a notification to her son or other caregiver.

**IoB will enable software to be more predictive about behavior changes.** With the troves of "big data" accumulating about behavior and wearables, this IoB enables the ability to predict future issues to become more sophisticated. Software associated with them will be able to correlate personal characteristics (like age, conditions, location) with environment, changes in individual behavior, and device accuracy (and/or failures). There will then be reasons to consider wearables across multiple older adult groups and needs. Marketing of these offerings will fit into the decade-old Design for All paradigm, promoting and enabling software customization based on user profile.

## Barriers to Wearables Adoption by Older Adults

As has been the case with many technology innovations that could benefit older adults, the concept may be good, but the implementation and/or data integration may be lacking. What might be the impediments limiting adoption of wearables? These include:

**Usability of the device and the data.** What stands between the data from a wearable and its use by providers and seniors? The Electronic Health Record (EHR) and the lack of interoperability among health systems present major obstacles—to date, the industry has not built the capability to capture data sent their way. And physicians, as the Forrester report noted, may not be interested in acquiring that data (or even worrisome alerts or signals from it) until systems can accommodate it and benefits have been proven. Usability also applies to text legibility on smartwatches; hearables and their dependency on smartphones; virtual reality technology and its dependency on headsets; and wearables that must be finely tuned for the individual.

> When you think about user design and experience, any friction in the interface should be removed. Tech that removes the screen is the best way to approach the digital divide.
>
> —Kyle Rand, CEO, **Rendever**

**Skepticism and concerns about health-related wearables.** Not just physicians—the older adult population may also be cautious. Considering the unanswered questions about wearables, including the need for calibration with other devices, the doubts expressed by the medical community, and the confusion about privacy defaults, it is not surprising that while vendors and experts are excited about the possibilities, there is a lack of awareness about them. And even if aware, there may be a lack of enthusiasm among the intended users. As with the "I'm Old" stigma about PERS devices, there may also be a stigma associated with health conditions.

> We're tackling the stigma associated with monitoring blood pressure. Education is a centerpiece. Half of U.S. adults are in the hypertensive range and the most significant rise in this condition is under the age of 45.
>
> —Jeff Ray, Executive Director of Business and Technology, **Omron Healthcare**

**Accuracy of measurements.** As noted, Remote Patient Monitoring (RPM) is one example of a wearable combined with other technologies to remotely monitor patients with chronic (or post-discharge) conditions. While telehealth took off during the pandemic, for example, it has returned to being just one tool in the toolkit for physicians, depending on the willingness of the patient and difficulty of getting to in-person appointments. Wearables will similarly be incorporated into processes with some caution on the part of healthcare providers.

> With a wearable, data is available 24x7, but it must be filtered and managed properly to make actionable.
>
> —Rod Cruz, GM Healthcare **AT&T Business**

**Actionability.** The healthcare industry has deployed systems that produced so many alerts, practitioners began to ignore them, complaining of alert fatigue. As a result, it is no surprise today if they resist data integration from wearables. But personalized consumer wearables are different. Looking down at a wrist worn device that says "Stand!" may prompt movement from a chair. Given the opportunity to respond to a nudge, we may or may not act, but at least a visible suggestion is made that enables action.

> The digital convenience in our consumer lives doesn't make it into health and care. Yet we want to participate in our care—and wearables enable co-producing data that could lead to better outcomes.
> —Karsten Russell-Wood,
> Portfolio Leader, Post-Acute and Home, **Philips**

**Willingness and ability to use.** As devices evolve into lighter and simpler form factors, will older adults, including the oldest, wear them? They just might, armed with information and encouragement from peers, families, physical therapists, or caregivers. With the emergence of rings, bands, patches, and cheap smartwatches like the $20 Wyze band announced in December 2020, unobtrusive wearables may become a symbol of high-quality self- or professional care.

> The future of healthcare is here. Today's super-watches are complete smartphones on our wrists—with fall detection, health and wellness tracking, communications, news, weather, and more, in beautiful stylish designs.
> —Mark Gray, CEO, **Constant Companion**

**Privacy concerns.** As with the advent of always-listening smart speakers, all ages should be concerned about what is done with the data from wearables—who gets it, how is it monetized, and what steps can be taken to rein in the tech company instinct to add or deploy features without informing users. Consider the YouTube guidance about their policy, scrolling down to changing terms of service to see how little access or leverage an older adult has who is just watching a video sent by a home care aide, and how there is even less leverage for the home care provider.

> There often is a lack of transparency and inability of people to tailor how data are shared—consumers frequently don't have those

kinds of choices and can't always count on tech companies alone to protect the information.

— Deven McGraw, Chief Regulatory Officer, **Citizen**

# Future of Wearables and Older Adults

## *Personalized, Predictive, Proactive*

It's a bright future for the wearables market—predictions are optimistic, and interviewees for this report agreed with assertions that wearables are likely to become ever more:

**SMART: Tracking behaviors that can predict decline or health status.** The monitoring capabilities of wearables are only now beginning to be used in caring for older adults—with tech offerings from multiple firms, either as research experiments or for actual usage. In the future, the identification band worn in senior living communities and nursing homes could be a smart band with ID information, medications, and allergies, as part of a GPS-trackable tag, particularly useful in dementia care. Firms that provide care for older adults will evaluate health-related wearables for care recipients who have specific health conditions, and some will provide their services as a subscription offering that could include personalized advice or alerts.

> We are going to be a cloud of data points—and it will be aggregated onto a wearable because it is an all-in-one device. Ultimately this will be a data play and the model will evolve to a monthly subscription, perhaps combining various elements of care like concierge services with health & wellness coaching.
>
> —Satish Movva, CEO and Founder, **CarePredict**

INTEGRATED: **With other devices fed into health profiles.** For the time being, those health profiles may be Personal Health Records (PHRs). Or a report could be printed, as one interviewee noted is happening today, and attached as a PDF to the record. One way or another, data that is not captured someplace else, like blood pressure trends, blood sugar levels, gait, or history of falls will all need to find its way into health-related guidance or into a data set that is queried with AI tools to look for trends or issues that the patient did not mention.

AFFORDABLE: **For lower-income seniors needing hearing help or smartwatches.** The change in prices of hearing assistance will come from availability and quality of hearables, the rise of self-service hearing assessment tools, and the long-delayed FDA approval of over-the-counter hearing aids. Worried users will take one of many online hearing tests or walk up to an in-store kiosk. The range of easily purchased and no-stigma in-ear hearables will be widespread. And the next generation of low-priced smartwatches of the future, coupled with a 24/7 service subscription, will replace the low-priced PERS offerings sold in retail stores.

PROTECTIVE: **Of your privacy.** Wearables transmit the most personal (and personalized) information tech users have. The ability to protect privacy—requiring explicit opt-in permission for data or Amazon network sharing—means that information protection principles, known as Privacy by Design, should and will be expected by users, even where they are not mandated by law. And changes in terms about that privacy will be communicated in easy-to-understand terms, requiring the user to again acknowledge that they have seen the change.

PRESCRIBED: **Utility of wearables will transcend practitioner reluctance to prescribe**. More Medicare Advantage plans could reimburse the cost of a wearable for certain patient groups. For example, Fitbit devices are currently included in Medicare Advantage plans offered by insurers. Devoted Health was the first Medicare Advantage plan to subsidize an Apple Watch, though Aetna Attain provides a health incentive for an Apple Watch—and others will follow. With health insurer pressure, eventually the "doctors don't want your data" mantra will end.

> As older adults become more comfortable using technology, senior living providers see that they may need to add "tech concierge" support staff to handle tech support needs from residents and staff.
> —Jessica Longly, **CDW Healthcare**

## Beyond Five Years: What Wearables Will Mean for Seniors

**Smartphone link requirements will be optional.** The out-of-the-box wearable will offer choices for registration and continued data collection. Caregivers can set them up on behalf of an older adult—who will confirm that permission to collect data has been explicitly provided. The wearer can deny access to the data (steps and heart rate, for example) to family—but

**Table 3.1 The Future of Wearables and Older Adults—Within Five Years.**

| WHAT | From | To |
|---|---|---|
| Mode of wear | Predominantly wrist, ear, device-specific, user-integrated | Multiple body areas, patches, rings, data-integrated |
| Interaction method | Primarily touch | Touchless, voice |
| Chronic disease management | Diabetes, hearing loss, cardiac | Integrated across diseases |
| Safety monitoring | Falls, user-signaled, with/without location | Multiple risks, location tracked |
| Intervention feedback | Episodic, when checked | Continuously available, alerted if out of range |
| Role of sleep | Device-specific monitoring | Multiple monitors, in combination |
| Hearing health, measurement | Hearing aid, audiologist serviced | Hearables-centric, self-service |
| Cost/availability | Consumer-paid | Insurance-covered |
| Physician recommendation | Suggested | Prescribed |
| Privacy management | Default opt-in assumed | Required opt-in |
| Location of health monitoring | At healthcare provider location | At home, self-monitoring, alerting |

subscribe to spoken advice from the wearable itself. "You walked much more today, maybe you'd like a piece of chocolate as a snack!" The wearer is intrigued, and signs up for MyFitnessPal to begin tracking exercise plus food calories and weight.

**Voice interaction with wearables will be a required feature.** The wonder of wearables is that they are unobtrusive AND have multiple uses, thus are less likely to be left behind on a bedside table. Individuals with vision limitations or dexterity issues will find wearable interaction daunting, even annoying without voice-based access. Bulky wearables with touchy glass surfaces will give way to slimline form factors with voice links. Senior living marketers will get it—and offer seniors with Parkinson's tremor or arthritis these just-for-them devices when they decide to move in. Home care companies will use "free" wearables as an enticement to caregivers, as well as prospective care recipients.

> Based on an individual's physical limitations, the best products will have an option for voice or even voice-only access and AI within a wearable can assist with verbal presentation.
> —Ray Spoljaric, CEO, **Aloe Care Health**

**Identity wearable tags in the senior living industry will all be smart tags.** GPS tracking of seniors with dementia will enable more freedom on senior living properties. Health information will be stored as well, scannable in emergency rooms, transmitting a list of conditions and allergies for those with cognitive impairment who may arrive alone in an ambulance. Seniors who fall will have instantaneous notification of caregivers or emergency services, eliminating disabling or fatal long lie times. Gait analysis of older adults will be available to an individual's care circle, enabling wellbeing interventions to begin before frailty level worsens.

**Integrated health-aware wearables will make suggestions to coach, improve outcomes.** In addition to piping up with suggestions, smartwatches will be able to prompt about food choices and medication reminders. Seniors will see/hear a suggestion to request a prescription refill on the appropriate date. Medication non-adherence will decline for smartwatch owners. Related adverse health incidents will decline. Insurers will take notice and reward the consumer with gift cards or rate discounts.

> Imagine—Mrs. Jones takes a statin. If a technology you took to the grocery store "knew" you were taking a statin, it would scan products and say, "don't buy that grapefruit juice." People plus data—give away the device. The real value is in the data. Get the consumer's opt-in, provide a value exchange.
> —Jane Sarasohn-Kahn, **THINK-Health and Health Populi blog**

## Resources

**AARP 2021 Tech Trends and the 50+**
**Advances in Healthcare Wearables, April 2021**
**Consumer Technology Association: 2020 Guidance for Wearable Health Tech**

Forrester Research: Wearables are for Consumers, Not Doctors,
   April 2021
Gartner: Top Strategic Trends for 2021
Gartner: Global Spending on Wearable Devices to Total $81.5
   Billion in 2021
IDC: Wearable Devices Forecasts 28.4% Market Growth
Pew Research FactTank: One in Five Americans Use a Smartwatch
   or Wearable
PubMed: Using Fitness Trackers and Smartwatches to Measure
   Physical Activity
RoboticsBiz: Smart Sensors, Key Components and Advantages,
   May 2021
TripleTree: A New Era of Virtual Health, April 2021
Wearable Device Adoption by Older Adults, December 2020
Wearable Technology in 2021: Five Burning Questions
   Cardiologists are Asking

## About Laurie M. Orlov

Laurie M. Orlov, a tech industry veteran, writer, speaker, and elder care
advocate, is the founder of Aging and Health Technology Watch, which
provides market research, trends, blogs, and reports that provide thought
leadership, analysis, and guidance about health- and aging-related technologies and services that enable boomers and seniors to sustain and improve
their quality of life. In her previous career, Laurie spent many years in the
technology industry, including nine years at analyst firm Forrester Research.
She has spoken regularly and delivered keynote speeches at forums, industry consortia, conferences, and symposia, most recently on the business
of technology for boomers and seniors. She advises large organizations
as well as non-profits and entrepreneurs about trends and opportunities
in the age-related technology market. Her segmentation of this emerging
technology market and trends commentary have been presented in the
Journal of Geriatric Care Management. Her perspectives have been quoted
in Business Week, CNBC, Forbes, Kiplinger, NPR, the Wall Street Journal,
and the New York Times. She has a graduate certification in Geriatric Care
Management from the University of Florida and a BA in Music from the
University of Rochester. Advisory clients have included AARP, Argentum,
Microsoft, Novartis, J&J, United Healthcare, CDW Healthcare, Bose, Cox
Communications, and Philips. Her latest reports include the **2021 Market**

**Overview of Technology for Aging**, **The Future of Remote Care Technology and Older Adults 2020**, **Voice, Health and Wellbeing 2020**, and **The Future of Voice First Technology and Older Adults (2018)**. Laurie has been named one of the **Top 50 Influencers in Aging by Next Avenue** and one of the **Women leading global innovation on Age Tech**.

## Firms That Provided Insights for This Chapter

| | |
|---|---|
| AARP | Jewish Senior Living Group |
| Alango Technologies | LiveFreely |
| Aloe Care Health | MobileHelp |
| Alva Health | Omron Healthcare |
| AT&T Business | Ōura Ring |
| CarePredict | Paul Barter & Associates |
| CDW Healthcare | Philips Healthcare |
| CIITIZEN | Rendever |
| Consumer Technology Association | Samsung |
| Constant Companion | THINK-Health |
| EchoWear | Thrive Well |
| Fitbit | UnaliWear |
| Hands-Free Health | Valencell |
| FallCall Solutions | |

# Chapter 4

# Home Care and Wellness

Michael W. Davis

## Contents

## Smart Speakers Becoming Healthcare Monitors

### The Problem: A Multitude of Remote Patient Monitoring Devices May Impact Compliance

Remote patient monitoring (RPM) may require patients to acquire various medical monitoring devices that can be attached to provide clinical data or that are worn to provide continuous patient monitoring. Patients might be required to have monitoring devices for blood pressure, oxygen saturation, heart rate, temperature, weight, or cardiac rhythms. Patients with multiple chronic disease issues or comorbidities may require the use of several of

DOI: 10.4324/9781003304036-5

these monitoring devices. Older patients may find hooking these devices up for monitoring to be a challenge, and that could lead to noncompliance challenges for RPM. If patients do not have access to reliable internet communications, then the ability for patients to use mobile or cellular communications may impact RPM compliance. This can be challenging for patients in rural localities.

Multiple device use for patients may be challenging for hooking the devices up to a hub system that transmits the results to the providers. If different devices require different connection processes, patients may become confused and frustrated, and that will impact the expected healthcare outcomes.

The need for multiple devices to support RPM services will also be challenging for providers. More devices result in higher support overhead and maintenance costs. Different RPM solutions may also use different communication protocols, which may also be challenging and expensive to maintain. Replacement and technology obsolescence costs should also be a consideration for providers regarding RPM solutions. RPM technologies are changing rapidly.

## The Solution: Smart Speakers Continue to Advance Home Health RPM Capabilities

Amazon Echo and Google Home are advancing technologies that will allow their smart speakers to monitor your heartbeat without any physical contact. Both regular and irregular heart rhythms can be identified using a two-factor algorithm. As smart speaker RPM capabilities continue to advance, they represent a great way for providers to create an intuitive and cost-effective approach to provide homecare that is emerging to improve patient satisfaction and care quality.

In a recent blog, I identified a new standard for connecting appliances to smart home devices that is being supported by Apple, Google, Amazon, and Zigbee. This new standard is called Connected Home over IP (CHIP). The support of these large technology companies, all of whom provide smart home/speaker devices, will continue to drive more advanced RPM services for their solutions. These companies also provide leading voice recognition solutions that may be advanced to use voice biometrics to generate additional RPM capabilities.

Amazon, Google, and Apple advancing RPM solutions via their smart home/speaker solutions will have a significant impact on the RPM market over time. The presence of these companies will drive market consolidation for RPM. This may drive down RPM costs and improve interoperability between these smart speaker solutions and provider EHRs.

One downside for using smart home/speaker solutions for RPM is that it will only apply to the middle- or higher-income socioeconomic groups, unless the technology companies can drive down costs and make these solutions affordable to lower-income groups.

### The Justification: Higher Patient Satisfaction and Compliance with RPM Solutions

The ability to use smart home/speaker solutions to support RPM processes is further enhanced by the ability of these devices to suggest medication refills, provide symptom-checker services, and remind patients of upcoming scheduled medical events. Smart home/speaker solutions are some of the most advanced voice recognition systems in use today. The sophistication of these solutions enables consumers to easily interact with these products to perform a number of personal service functions that help to manage their day-to-day activities. Adding healthcare services to these environments will provide a powerful tool to help providers and payers better manage their patient populations and, more specifically, to manage their high-risk populations.

### The Players: The Big Three Will Continue to Dominate the Market

Amazon, Google, and Apple competition will continue to drive higher levels of healthcare capabilities for their smart home/speaker solutions. It will be interesting to see how long it takes for Apple and Google to link the smart home/speaker devices to their associated smartphones. This will ensure patients are always connected to these services.

- Amazon Echo
- Google Home
- Apple Home

### Success Factors

1. Provider organizations should begin to establish RPM strategies that include smart home/speaker solutions to supplement their current services.

2. Patient populations where smart home/speaker devices could improve RPM services and quality of care should be identified for prototype testing.
3. The ability to link smart home/speaker devices with smartphones and smartwatches should also be evaluated for longer-term RPM impacts.

## Summary

Smart home/speaker devices represent a disruptive technology for providing or supplementing RPM services. Amazon, Google, and Apple are large companies that are likely to continue to leverage smart device healthcare services that will improve consumer healthcare. These companies can also expand their services by linking smart home/speaker devices with smartphones and smartwatches. This will provide the ability to continually monitor and manage patients during their daily activities. These solutions are based on voice recognition technologies that will drive quick consumer adoption and higher levels of patient satisfaction.

The keys to success for smart home/speaker solutions are the ability to interoperate with provider EHR systems via standards such as FHIR and the ability to extend voice-supported healthcare services to smartphones and smartwatches to improve the ability of low-income consumers to participate in these services.

Once we have consumers driving higher levels of market share for voice-enabled healthcare services from smart devices, how long will it be before healthcare professionals are demanding the same technology capabilities from their financial and clinical applications?

# Chapter 5

# Telehealth

Michael W. Davis

## Contents

DOI: 10.4324/9781003304036-6

## Telehealth Continues to Advance in High-Risk Market

### The Problem: Telehealth Version 1.0—Lots of Players, Little Differentiation

COVID-19 has forever changed primary healthcare delivery. To survive financially, physicians had to quickly learn and implement a telehealth solution to deliver virtual care. The catalyst for implementing telehealth services was the Medicare 1135 waiver that reimbursed telehealth visits at the same rate as office visits[1]. This waiver was created to ensure patients would not be needlessly exposed to COVID-19 during an office visit.

The new CMS reimbursement guidelines opened the payment floodgates. Currently, there are over 260 telehealth vendors[2]. This high number of vendors manifests the low barriers of entry to creating a solution in this market. Further confounding the market is the high market value placed on the Teladoc and Livongo merger[3]. How can the merger of two companies with negative EBITDA values be worth a combined $37 billion? What differentiates Teladoc from the other telehealth solutions, beyond their first mover market advantage? The telehealth market will be extremely competitive, and several companies will advance to compete for market leadership flush with investor cash. This success of this merger will also be challenged by the EHR vendors who are extending their portfolios to include telehealth capabilities[4]. The other key question is how easy is it to replace telehealth solutions? If an organization implemented telehealth for the COVID-19 emergency, will it replace those products with solutions provided by their EHR vendors or more robust solutions?

## The Solution: Telehealth That Is Flexible and Extensible

As the healthcare organizations move forward with implementing virtual healthcare delivery service models, the ability of the telehealth platform to extend these services across socio-economic environments of patient populations will be critical for long-term success. If patients do not have the internet or smartphones, how will healthcare organizations provide telehealth services? One emerging solution is to use televisions[5]. In some areas, cable companies will begin to convert their cable boxes into smart home devices that compete with Amazon's Alexa or Google Home. Telehealth companies that can easily integrate their platforms into the smart home devices with FHIR APIs are likely to become market leaders.

The ability of telehealth solutions to integrate a range of disease management guidelines to share with virtual care patients so they can more effectively manage their own care will also differentiate these products. The ability to use disease management content from respected sources such as Mayo, WebMD, Cleveland Clinic, and others delivers the flexibility that most providers desire as they develop their virtual care services.

Remote patient monitoring and wearables integration will be needed by telehealth solutions to establish a treatment environment that is equivalent to in-clinic visits. Capturing key vital signs such as blood pressure, pulse, pulse oximeter, weight, and temperature before, during, and after the telehealth encounters will enable more effective provider management of the patient. Smartwatches are also emerging that can collect several key vital sign measures as well as EKG tracings[6] that can be shared via Bluetooth connections with telehealth and EHR solutions.

## The Justification: Telehealth Is the Foundation for Patient-Focused Care

In most cases, patients will not likely revert to the primary care model where they must travel to physician clinics to receive their care. Recent survey results showed that nearly three-quarters of patients who experience telehealth services were highly satisfied[7]. Healthcare organizations that design telehealth services to integrate with EHR and population health management applications will improve care coordination and outcomes. Telehealth services will need to be integrated into patient access platforms for scheduling the service, as well as registration functions for identifying insurance and pertinent demographic information. These patient access functions should be a component of patient portals to further enhance the virtual care experience.

## The Players: Established and Emerging Vendors Compete in an Immature Market

While the Teladoc/Livongo merger is front and center now, representative key competitors will come from EHR, telecommunications, and technology companies:

- Verizon Telehealth Services—https://enterprise.verizon.com/solutions/public-sector/telehealth/
- Epic Systems—www.healthcareitnews.com/news/epic-launches-new-telehealth-service-twilio
- Zoom—https://zoom.us/healthcare
- Microsoft—www.microsoft.com/en-us/microsoft-365/microsoft-teams/healthcare-solutions
- Teladoc—www.teladoc.com/
- SecureVideo—www.securevideo.com/
- Amwell—https://business.amwell.com/

Large technology and telecommunications vendors have the capital and market reach to become dominant players in the telehealth market. But non-healthcare focused companies have struggled in the past to provide well supported and designed healthcare products.

## Success Factors

- Select a proven telehealth platform that has been implemented in several healthcare modalities of care to prove its capabilities.
- Integrate the telehealth solution with the EHR, population health, and patient portal applications to enable optimum coordinated care services.
- Integrate remote patient monitoring devices and wearable appliances to deliver timely vital sign data that effectively supports the telehealth encounter.

## Summary

The US telehealth market is immature and constitutes a high risk for both providers and vendors. It is relatively easy to create a HIPAA-compliant audio/video solution that can support provider/patient healthcare encounters. COVID-19 and relaxed reimbursement regulations for telehealth resulted in many provider organizations implementing products that may not be good long-term solutions. If this is true, the market will experience a high degree of telehealth replacement activity over the next year. Solutions offered by telecommunications, technology, EHR, and audio/visual conference vendors will create a highly competitive market for providers to evaluate for their next version of telehealth. Telehealth vendors that can extend their solutions via integration with smart home devices and remote patient monitoring devices, including wearables, will be best positioned to optimize telehealth services for providers. First mover market advantage for some telehealth vendors will not be a competitive barrier to the well capitalized and technologically advanced competitors that are emerging. "Number 1: Cash is king. Number 2: Communicate. Number 3: Buy or bury the competition." —Jack Welch

# The Transformation of Primary Care and the Digital Technology Catalyst

## The Problem: COVID-19 Exposes Gaps in Primary Care Systems

The US healthcare system is one of the highest-cost environments in the world. But the high cost does not translate to better outcomes or healthcare quality. In 2019, the US ranked 30 out of 89 countries measured by the WHO for factors that contribute to overall health[8]. US healthcare spending was $3.6 trillion or $11,172 per person in 2018[9]. Healthcare represented 17.7 percent of the US GDP in 2018.

The US healthcare system has created one of the greatest inequities in the world for its citizens to access affordable healthcare. This issue was magnified by COVID-19, as the ability to deliver effective care and pandemic surveillance monitoring drove healthcare organizations to quickly adapt telehealth and other digital technologies to deliver primary care and remotely monitor patients. In many cases, the use of immature or first version telehealth solutions was lacking in needed functionality (especially remote patient monitoring), but healthcare organizations implemented solutions that met their needs. Primary care physicians needed to create revenue streams to support their clinics. "Necessity is the mother of invention," and physicians quickly learned to use telehealth and other digital technologies to survive. Telehealth adoption was not a high growth technology market before the virus, but has emerged as a high growth healthcare technology segment since March 2020. Telehealth growth in 2020 is expected to rise 65%[10]. Much of this growth is also related to CMS adopting higher levels of reimbursement for telehealth.

## The Solution: Telehealth, Remote Patient Monitoring, and Digital Patient Engagement Are Transformers

Once patients experienced telehealth services, they quickly realized they could receive care in the convenience of their homes. They no longer had to drive to a clinic (perhaps several miles away in bad traffic) or be exposed to other sick patients in the clinic waiting rooms. The emergence of remote monitoring devices and wearables also improved the ability of clinicians to monitor the health status of high-risk patients. Remote patient monitoring provided by smartwatches and solutions from companies such as Rimidi[11] are evolving to close the gap in telehealth services for matching the efficacy of clinic visits. Patient engagement services supported by application devices for scheduling primary care, accessing care guidance instructions, reviewing a personal health record, conducting medication refills, and directly communicating with care providers via email or text messaging are functional examples that need to be integrated into all provider patient portals.

Retail healthcare services are also quickly emerging that will support lower-level primary care services with increased convenience for access and much lower service costs. Walmart, Walgreens, and CVS are quickly driving more convenient and affordable healthcare services for consumers. These companies will be using digital technologies to deliver their new primary care services.

Another company to watch is RO[12]. RO just received $200 million in additional funding to continue to grow their remote and home care services. Digital service capabilities will now be the focus of healthcare providers to meet consumer demand. The number of healthcare organization clinics will decline.

## The Justification: Patient-Focused Healthcare Rules

Digital technologies supporting primary care have established a new model for delivering services that truly meet the needs of most patients. These technologies are driving new methods for delivering and support-ing patient care from emerging vendors and from retail healthcare giants. Patient-focused healthcare is no longer just a platitude espoused by health-care organizations; it is now the platform that will ensure long-term viabil-ity for the provider organizations who can successfully implement these emerging primary care models. Digital technologies that extend telehealth, remote patient monitoring, and patient engagement services will be a required component of healthcare organization strategies moving forward. Perhaps unnecessary clinics can be sold to help fund digital technology implementations.

## The Players: Emerging Companies and Retail Health

The vendors that use digital technology platforms to provide primary care services are represented by the following companies:

- RO Health—https://ro.co/
- Lemonaid Health—www.lemonaidhealth.com/
- Walgreens Clinics—www.walgreens.com/pharmacy/healthcare-clinic.jsp
- Walmart Clinics—www.walmart.com/cp/care-clinics/1224932
- CVS Minute Clinics—www.cvs.com/minuteclinic

Healthcare organizations that cannot provide competitive digital services with these companies are likely to lose most of their primary care service markets.

## Success Factors

- Evaluate telehealth solutions relative to intuitive design for both physicians and patients for easy access and operations.
- Investigate the ability of the telehealth solution to integrate remote patient monitoring devices and/or wearables into the environment to better support the telehealth encounter.
- Expand patient engagement services to enhance the ability to schedule and prepare for telehealth services with required treatment guidelines and instructions.

## Summary

COVID-19 has been both a disaster and blessing to US healthcare. The blessing emerged in the form of primary care physicians adopting telehealth and other digital health services to provide basic and preventive care services to patients who were restricted in their ability to travel outside their homes. Patients receiving remote care services are unlikely to revert to the old care paradigm of traveling to a clinic to receive most primary care. The continuing advancement of technologies such as smartwatches, speech recognition (e.g., ability to recognize people who may have COVID-19 from their voice patterns), and mobile applications that can be used to help consumers identify potential health issues and provide corresponding treatment guidance and physician connections, will add an additional layer of capabilities to digital health capabilities. Healthcare organizations need to continue to focus on extending their digital healthcare services to remain competitive in the primary care markets. Time to put on your sunglasses. The patient-focused future looks bright.

# In-Home Care—Complementing Remote Patient Monitoring

## The Problem: Supporting the Last Mile of Patient-Focused Care

Some chronically ill patients may not have the ability or resources to trek to an urgent care center or a medical clinic to receive more advanced care that can be provided via telehealth. The US also has a reimbursement issue relative to in-home care reimbursement,[13] but this could be eliminated as the COVID-19 service/outcomes analysis identifies benefits of the approach.

Being able to treat people in their homes is a key foundation for patient-focused healthcare. The ability of care providers to visit patients in their homes provides a level of care beyond telehealth that may be necessary to truly determine the health of a patient. As the industry moves to higher levels of care reimbursement based on value, it will be important to have in-home care services to support higher levels of outcomes for chronic diseases, fragile health, and end-of-life services.

The coordination of services that include dietary support, diagnostic testing, medication management, physical therapy, respiratory therapy, and dialysis is challenging for many providers who do not coordinate in-home care as part of their network services. If providers are not providing in-home services, they may be losing revenue to emerging in-home care services that offer physician and advanced practice provider visits on demand. If in-home care services become an extension of retail health providers (e.g., Walgreens, Walmart, and CVS), provider networks will have a significant new threat to their current business models.

## The Solution: Moving More Patient Care to Home Delivery

Providing in-home care using physicians and advanced practice providers delivers another level of patient-focused care that is driving new players into the market funded by established venture capital companies.[14] Mayo Clinic represents a provider network that understands the need to extend care to patients' homes via telehealth.[15] Mayo Clinic is using a partnership with Medically Home as a foundation of this service. Mayo Clinic is also using AI-based solutions to drive these services to new levels of capabilities.

In-home care can deliver five key benefits: (1) a choice for patients relative to care delivery that can be provided in the home environment, (2) proximity to family and friends to improve care support, (3) cost efficiencies for patients and their support network, (4) a likely decrease in hospital readmissions, and (5) the ability to maintain a quality of life.[16]

The emergence of digital technologies that can accurately and efficiently monitor clinical data relative to a patient's health will continue to evolve to better enable effective in-home care. As the patient data is captured, emerging AI applications can evaluate the data to determine what interventions may be needed to ensure the best possible patient outcomes. Over time, smartwatches may be the only patient-monitoring device needed for most patients receiving in-home care.[17]

## The Justification: Less Costly Patient Care Services

The cost effectiveness of in-home care has been shown in several studies.[18] In-home oxygen therapy, blood glucose monitoring, heart failure treatments, and intravenous antibiotic therapy have all been shown to drive cost reductions for healthcare delivery services. The ability to reduce care delivery costs and improve outcomes will be a requirement for the viability of healthcare providers as the market moves to higher levels of value-based care reimbursements. Healthcare providers who first demonstrate market-moving advantages in their markets for efficient and high-quality in-home care services will be the best positioned for long-term viability.

## The Players: Innovative Providers and Emerging Vendor Solutions

Innovative healthcare provider organizations have realized the advantages and need for extending care delivery to the patient's home. In some cases, emerging vendors are establishing services outside of provider networks because this service need is not being provided by providers in the patient's network or service area. Representative solution providers are the following:

- Mayo Clinic
- Medically Home
- DispatchHealth

## Success Factors

- Third-party in-home care solutions should demonstrate interoperability with a provider's EHR or population health systems.
- The ability to monitor patients' clinical data remotely in a timely manner for the services being supplied needs to be proven.
- Self-developed solutions created by extending EHR or telehealth solutions need to deliver proven remote patient monitoring and care plans that are interoperable with EHRs or population heath applications.

## Summary

In-home care is emerging as both an asynchronous (set up visit as needed) and a synchronous solution (an extension of EHR and population health interventions). Healthcare organizations should begin to establish strategies for extending telehealth services to in-home care services to reduce care costs and improve patient outcomes. The ability to collect in-home care information for sharing with primary care and specialty care physicians, whether from an asynchronous or a synchronous care episode, is a critical success factor with these services. In-home solutions will require intuitive and integrated patient-monitoring devices, as well as AI environments that are used to continually improve patient care plans and diagnostic decision support.

If emerging retail health services (e.g., Walmart, CVS, or Walgreens) extend their services with in-home healthcare, a significant market disruption is likely to occur. The processes and technology involved in extending services to in-home care are relatively straightforward in most cases and require no use of provider care facilities. Pity the CFO of the poor provider organization with all the sunk-cost patient care facilities. As it was once said, "Pity for the guilty is treason to the innocent."—Terry Goodkind

# Wearable Technology Is Emerging as a Key RPM Strategy

## The Problem: Improving Healthcare Quality for Episodes of Virtual Care

As healthcare reimbursement moves toward higher adoption of value-based care (VBC)[19], the ability to effectively monitor and manage high-risk patients becomes a critical factor for organization viability. The fee for service (FFS) reimbursement model focuses on managing patients that optimize the care delivery environments of the provider. In most cases, patients must travel to primary care clinics, or to specialty clinics to receive care in the FFS model. While this model may optimize the utilization capacity of the provider's care facilities, it does little to facilitate care that accommodates the patients' needs.

COVID-19 created a "woke" environment for all healthcare stakeholders for care delivery needs and innovative models. Telehealth became a key requirement for primary care physicians to not only render safe care, but to support revenue streams. New models of care delivery are patient-focused and determine care delivery services based on patient need. In some cases, telehealth will best support the patient encounter, or homecare might be the best option if patients need human interventions, or patients may still be willing and able to receive care in the clinic. As we move forward with more patient-focused care based on high-risk patients in at-risk contracts, it will be important to integrate remote patient monitoring (RPM) into care delivery services. It will also be important to use RPM solutions that are intuitive for patients to use and easy to integrate into care delivery data flows.

## The Solution: Wearable Technology—Evolving with a Wide Range of Clinical Monitoring

Over the last several months, wearable technology has evolved to monitor several clinical factors of the wearers. The Apple Watch and Fitbit monitor heart rate, irregular rhythms, and can provide an ECG reading to identify potential atrial fibrillation[20] [21]. If cardiologists prescribe these watches to their high-risk cardiology patients, how many readmissions will be avoided? How many ED visits will be avoided? An avoidance of either of these incidents can easily pay for the watch. The ability to capture consistent and timely patient readings for evaluation and assessment with other EHR data will improve the quality and safety of care. This data can also be combined in data analytics environments to monitor and/or create evidence-based medicine protocols. A wearable device will likely be more convenient and comfortable for the patient than using RPMs that must be worn on other parts of the body.

Other vital signs that can be monitored by wearables are blood pressure (Omron HealthGuide[22]), and stress indicators (Fitbit Versa 3[23]). Some of these wearables also have temperature and oxygen saturation sensors, which are key vital signs for monitoring COVID-19 infections.

Wearable technologies are advancing their ability to monitor, report, and track key patient vital signs. As these technologies continue to improve, we would also expect the cost of these solutions to decline. This scenario supports a defensible ROI of these devices to support healthcare delivery services to high-risk patients.

## The Justification: What Is the Cost of a Readmission or ED Visit?

In 2016, the average cost of a hospital readmission across all principal diagnoses was $14,000, and the highest readmission rates were for patients on Medicare[24]. As healthcare reimbursement continues to move to higher rates of VBC, organizations must adopt virtual care models with RPM technologies to provide more efficient, effective, and lower-cost care to high-risk patients.

Most wearable devices are around $300 to buy. The prevention of one readmission is equal to approximately 46 wearable devices. Continue the math for an organization based on their true readmission rates to establish the potential cost savings for high-risk patients for one disease state or many.

## The Players: Big Tech Plus RPM-Focused Companies

Representative wearable solutions that are designed to be worn on the wrist are listed here. Other wearables that may be considered are those that include glasses and headsets.

- Google/Fitbit—www.fitbit.com/global/us/home
- Apple Watch—www.apple.com/watch/
- Samsung—www.samsung.com/us/watches/galaxy-watch3/
- Xiaomi—www.wareable.com/xiaomi
- Garmin—https://buy.garmin.com/en-US/US/wearabletech/wearables/c10001-c10002-p1.html
- Empatica—www.empatica.com/
- Spry Health—https://spryhealth.com/

At this time, the Apple Watch appears to be the most advanced solution, but Google/Fitbit and Samsung will continue to provide competitive pressure to drive advancement of these solutions.

## Success Factors

- If possible, lease these devices to provide protection from technological obsolescence. This technology advances in months, not years.
- Select devices that will either transmit patient data to secure cloud databases for downloading to the EHR, or that can connect to the EHR with cellular connections that support IoT devices.
- Monitor patient data received from wearable devices to analyze improvements to outcomes as well as healthcare cost reductions. Report the findings to executive management monthly.

## Summary

COVID-19, VBC, and patient-focused care are driving healthcare provider organizations to create new virtual care delivery models. As VBC reimbursement will be driven by outcomes and patient satisfaction, it is crucial to create healthcare services that support the socio-economic and lifestyle needs of patients. This becomes more evident when high-risk patient populations are analyzed to determine the best modalities for delivering efficient, safe, high-quality, and lower-cost care to minimize contact risk exposure.

The ability to incorporate wearable RPM solutions to support telehealth, home care, and population/disease management will enable providers to have a timely picture of the patient's healthcare status, which facilitates better care management. The ability to capture consistent streams of patient vital sign data will also improve data analytics used to create and manage care protocols.

In the next two to three years, you may see the smart wearable devices interoperate with smart home devices for the collection, management, and evaluation of data. This will likely result in real-time patient guidance and alerts that will improve both patient care and patient satisfaction.

## RESEARCH FRONTIERS DRIVING NEW HEALTHCARE WEARABLES AND SMARTPHONE CAPABILITIES

### Will Printable Skin Monitors Become the Next RPM Devices?

#### Ensuring Patient Satisfaction and Compliance with Virtual Care/Telemedicine

Before COVID-19, the trend of consumers wearing digital monitors such as watches or fitness trackers was declining. The 2020 Accenture Consumer Digital Health Survey identified a drop in wearable technologies from 2018 to 2020[28]. In 2018, the use of wearables to monitor the health status of a patient was at 33 percent. By 2020 it had dropped to 18 percent. The pandemic exposed the need for digital technologies to support telemedicine and virtual office visits. The same survey identified 50 percent of consumers saying a bad digital experience ruins the entire experience.

There are several challenges for effectively implementing wearable technologies to support telemedicine[29]. Wearable devices may generate inconsistent and imprecise measurements; battery requirements can limit effectiveness of the devices; achieving FDA security certification; the devices can be expensive; and these devices may have a high technological obsolescence risk.

Patient acceptance challenges for using wearable devices evolve around comfort and ease of provisioning the device with a smartphone or home network to transmit results to the provider. An uncomfortable device to wear is a non-starter. Patients may also balk at using wearables that detract from their appearance. The inability to create an intuitive link between the wearable device and a smartphone or home network to share real-time data will also result in failure of adoption of the wearable device by patients and physicians.

## The Solution—Wearable Monitors

Imagine medical sensor circuits printed directly to the back of the hand that obtained sensor outputs equal to or better than conventional commercial monitoring devices. The sensors measured temperature, humidity, blood oxygen, heart rate, blood pressure, and electrophysiologic signals. These printed circuits were developed by Chinese research that solved all the challenges for applying the sensors to the skin[30]. These sensors can work for aged people as well as children, and the devices can be reused. They simply wash off with hot water when they are no longer needed, but remain in place if bathed with tepid water. Data transmission is accomplished via wireless network components[31]. Researchers believe the printed circuits will be recyclable for reprinting.

The unanswered questions related to skin printable wearables are related to cost, reliability, and availability. Will the skin wearable be able to compete in cost with a smartwatch? How reliable will these printable sensors be, and how long will they last? Where will the printable sensor be applied? The doctors' offices, the hospital? What equipment and reagents will be required, and how adaptable is the print process to office or hospital environments?

If the printable skin sensors work well, they could be amazingly effective for monitoring babies and children where other wearables might be challenging to maintain. The flexibility of printed skin wearables might even evoke new art forms. Designs from famous tattoo artists or even designers such as Calvin Klein could make this approach to wearables a fashion statement—or not.

## The Justification: Lifestyles Will Drive Adoption

Textiles are now being developed that use metal wires to create health monitoring that can be used in clothes or bedsheets[32]. While embedding remote monitoring capabilities into patient clothes will likely lead skin printable sensors into the market, the key for both approaches is providing a remote monitoring solution that does not inhibit the patient's lifestyle. Providing a solution that is worn as clothing or printed on the skin ensures the monitoring is continuous and, in most cases, not obvious to the patient. While remote monitoring solutions such as watches and clothing might be removed by the patient at times, this is less likely for skin printable sensors.

## The Players: Patch Monitors Evolving to Skin Printable Monitors

Patch sensors are the likely precursors for skin printed sensor monitors if the technology becomes commercially viable. Some representative companies providing patches to monitor patients are:

- Leaf Patient Monitoring System—provides pressure sensor monitoring to eliminate the risk of pressure injuries; www.sn-leaf.com/
- Seers bio patches—body-worn wireless bio patch that continuously measures ECG, heart rate, heart rate variability, activity, and respiration rate; https://seerstech.com/
- BioIntelliSense—FDA-cleared BioSticker™ on-body sensor to monitor respiratory rate, heart rate at rest, and skin temperature for COVID-19; https://biointellisense.com/

## Success Factors

- Skin printable monitors are in the early phases of testing for accuracy, reliability, and applicability. Organizations with innovation centers that have experience with highly immature technologies should evaluate how to advance this technology to commercial solutions.
- Innovation center partnerships on skin printable sensors may lead to the most rapid and cost-effective commercialization of this technology.
- Organizations who create commercially viable skin printable monitoring solutions will become a disruptive influence on the wearables monitoring market.

## Summary

Most of us are familiar with the commercial where the bank scans the heads of their customers, which implies they have some type of chip embedded to identify the customer. While this was humorous, it was also insightful relative to how technologies might be used in appropriate ways to help people monitor and manage their health. While wearables such as the Apple Watch are becoming viable remote patient monitors, the challenges for widespread use of these devices are cost and ongoing technical advancement (e.g., new versions of the watches annually). The ability to print a monitoring device on the patient's skin for the specific vital signs that the provider wants to monitor continuously provides disruptive potential for RPM devices and services. While challenges related to cost, application requirements (e.g., instruments and reagents), and reliability will need to be proven, the vision is certainly something we can all support. Please make my skin-printable monitor look like a Minion.

## Voice Biomarkers Become a Key Disease Detection Solution

### *The Problem: Inexpensive, Readily Available Biomarkers for Disease Identification*

COVID-19 became a catalyst for providing virtual healthcare delivery services. As the pandemic raged across the country, providers began to immediately implement the use of telemedicine solutions to connect with patients who needed care but were also at high risk for viral infections. One challenge for the early telemedicine sessions is that providers were in most cases not able to have the most recent patient vital signs that could support disease identification and management.

Challenges for collecting patient information to support virtual telemedicine sessions relates to the ability of the patient to operate remote patient monitoring devices. The operation includes the ability to connect the devices to a network or cell phone to capture the monitor results for transmission to the telemedicine session or the provider's EHR. The patient must also know how to effectively operate the remote patient monitoring device (e.g., blood pressure cuff, pulse oximeter, thermometer, etc.).

Another challenge for remote patient monitoring devices is the risk of technological obsolescence. Smartwatches are emerging as an effective RPM strategy, but the watchmakers continually upgrade the watches and add new monitoring functionality. The Apple Watch you have today may not be as effective or provide the range of monitoring services that next year's watch will have. But for some patients, shelling out $400 per year for a new watch may be prohibitive.

## The Solution: Voice/Speech Biomarkers Become the Ultimate RPM Services

The most natural method for capturing a patient's clinical status is via voice biomarkers. Biomarkers in a patient's speech are emerging as new ways to monitor illnesses using AI/machine learning, ranging from COVID-19[33] to Parkinson's disease[34] and pulmonary hypertension[35][36]. While voice biomarkers will not provide RPM capabilities for the basic vital signs, they are advancing to provide identification and diagnosis of patients with significant illness.

Snap just spent $70 million to acquire enterprise voice assistant developer Voca.ai which is working on voice biomarkers to identify COVID-19-infected patients[37]. Imagine having an AI voice biomarker component integrated with your call center phones or your telemedicine solutions that can actively monitor the patient for potential COVID-19 infection. Patients that have a positive result can then be tested to verify the COVID-19 infection. This approach will help to reduce the unnecessary testing of patients for COVID-19, which can help drive down healthcare costs for states and healthcare organizations.

Future implementations of voice biomarkers in call centers or 911 services could help to identify patients who are at risk for COVID-19 so first responders are appropriately protected. This application of voice biomarkers could also be used to alert first responders to patients with pulmonary hypertension, so they have the equipment and medications needed to effectively stabilize the patient. Advancing voice biomarkers to identify additional cardio-pulmonary and neurological disorders will provide an early warning system for managing high-risk patients more effectively.

## The Justification: Voice Becomes a Diagnostic Guidance Tool

While most remote patient monitoring devices provide data on specific vital signs to support patients with known chronic illness or disease, they do not provide insights or guidance to support diagnosing a patient or discovering a secondary condition. The power of AI-supported voice biomarkers is the ability to quickly and accurately identify patient conditions that are unknown or unexpected, and that can have a significant negative impact to the patient's health if not detected and treated quickly. The ability to integrate these tools into smartphones and call centers will provide an inexpensive and effective health screening function to further support virtual patient care.

## The Players: Embryonic Vendors May Become Disruptive Giants

Voice biomarkers are in the exceedingly early stages of research, testing, and commercialization. Most of these companies will end up being acquired by larger healthcare companies, as demonstrated by the recent acquisition of voca.ai.

- Salcit Technologies (India)—COVID-19 risk.
- voca.ai (Israel)—COVID-19 in test mode with Carnegie Mellon University.
- VocalisHealth (U.S.)—COVID-19 in test mode, and pulmonary hypertension testing with Mayo Clinic.

## Success Factors

- Organizations should thoroughly review and test the voice biomarker AI algorithms on patient populations that have confirmed diagnoses for the illnesses of interest.
- The ability for the voice biomarker applications to run on both iOS and Android platforms is essential to support high-quality patient engagement.
- Organizations who plan to use this technology in call centers need to confirm their telephony equipment can support voice biomarker AI solutions.

## Summary

Voice biomarkers as an AI solution have a tremendous potential to supplement virtual healthcare services. The ability to apply these solutions with smartphones, telemedicine audio, and call centers will create another level of healthcare management that will improve care quality and outcomes. The ability to identify potential chronic illnesses or patient conditions that can prove fatal from a patient's conversation with a care provider is likely to reduce deaths and expensive emergency or acute care.

As an example, the ability to identify a patient who has COVID-19 from a conversation should result in immediate quarantine procedures or hospital admission. Early identification of COVID-19 using this method will likely result in quicker contact tracing processes, and improved protection for care providers who may encounter the patient in transit to the hospital. The identification of patients with unknown pulmonary hypertension should reduce stroke and heart attack incidents.

The advancement and commercialization of voice biomarker AI solutions will deliver the next generation of healthcare diagnostic support. "Utterances are the new hashtags."—Albert Creixell, Partnerships Head, Amazon Alexa

## Bibliography

[1] www.cms.gov/newsroom/fact-sheets/medicare-telemedicine-health-care-provider-fact-sheet

[2] www.beckershospitalreview.com/lists/260-telehealth-companies-to-know-2020.html

[3] www.businessinsider.com/teladoc-livongo-merge-185-billion-dollar-deal-2020-8#

[4] www.healthcareitnews.com/news/epic-launches-new-telehealth-service-twilio

[5] www.healthcarefinancenews.com/news/new-telehealth-technology-uses-tv-set

[6] www.cnet.com/health/what-is-ekg/

[7] https://patientengagementhit.com/news/telehealth-patient-satisfaction-high-paves-path-for-future-access

[8] https://ceoworld.biz/2019/08/05/revealed-countries-with-the-best-health-care-systems-2019/

[9] www.cms.gov/Research-Statistics-Data-and-Systems/Statistics-Trends-and-Reports/NationalHealthExpendData/NationalHealthAccountsHistorical

[10] www.beckershospitalreview.com/telehealth/telehealth-to-grow-nearly-65-in-2020-report-finds.html

[11] https://rimidi.com/

[12] https://ro.co/

[13] https://khn.org/news/pandemic-forced-insurers-to-pay-for-in-home-treatments-will-they-disappear/

[14] https://medcitynews.com/2020/06/dispatchhealth-raises-135-8m-for-in-home-urgent-care/

[15] www.beckershospitalreview.com/digital-transformation/mayo-clinic-unveils-virtual-at-home-care-model-5-things-to-know.html

[16] www.heraldsun.com.au/feature/special-features/the-five-benefits-of-home-health-care/news-story/ef4f1a8d2b6ffc28f202579f12c12596

[17] https://klasresearch.com/resources/blogs/2020/05/13/etech-insight-smartwatches-becoming-sophisticated-health-monitoring-devices

[18] www.aahomecare.org/news/post/cost-effectiveness-of-homecare
[19] www.cms.gov/Medicare/Quality-Initiatives-Patient-Assessment-Instruments/Value-Based-Programs/Value-Based-Programs
[20] www.apple.com/healthcare/apple-watch/
[21] www.mobihealthnews.com/news/fitbit-s-ecg-app-gets-regulatory-clearance-us-and-european-union
[22] https://omronhealthcare.com/products/heartguide-wearable-blood-pressure-monitor-bp8000m/
[23] https://voicebot.ai/2020/08/25/fitbit-adds-google-assistant-to-new-versa-3-and-sense-smartwatches-keeps-alexa-option/
[24] www.hcup-us.ahrq.gov/reports/statbriefs/sb248-Hospital-Readmissions-2010-2016.jsp
[25] https://en.wikipedia.org/wiki/Continua_Health_Alliance
[26] www.cms.gov/Regulations-and-Guidance/Guidance/Interoperability/index
[27] https://arstechnica.com/gadgets/2019/12/apple-google-and-amazon-team-up-for-joint-smart-home-standard/
[28] www.accenture.com/us-en/insights/health/leaders-make-recent-digital-health-gains-last
[29] www.volersystems.com/pros-and-cons-of-wearable-technology-in-healthcare/
[30] www.acs.org/content/acs/en/pressroom/presspacs/2020/acs-presspac-october-14-2020/wearable-circuits-printed-directly-on-human-skin.html
[31] https://techxplore.com/news/2020-10-wearable-sensors-skin.html
[32] www.mouser.com/applications/healthcare-may-reside-in-smart-clothing/
[33] www.technologynetworks.com/diagnostics/news/signs-of-covid-19-may-be-hidden-in-speech-signals-vocal-biomarkers-new-findings-suggest-337639
[34] www.sciencedirect.com/science/article/abs/pii/S1532046419302825
[35] www.ncbi.nlm.nih.gov/pmc/articles/PMC7162478/
[36] https://medcitynews.com/2020/11/researchers-turn-an-ear-to-voice-based-biomarkers/
[37] https://voicebot.ai/2020/11/11/voice-tech-startup-voca-ai-acquired-by-snap-inc-for-70m-report/

## Chapter 6

# Remote Patient Monitoring (RPM)

Elias Lozano, Simon F. Meza, Adrian Alexander,
Paola Bonilla and Wilson Jaramillo

## Contents

DOI: 10.4324/9781003304036-7

# Introduction

## *Esvyda Origins*

During our early beginnings, and with our engineering background, Esvyda started to develop a complete platform that included connectivity of devices, onboarding registration of patients, Electronic Medical Records (EMR), vital signs collection from devices, reporting, billing, medication subscription/adherence, and others. It was an exciting time, since Esvyda's goal was to have an end-to-end HIPAA-compliant solution that did not require other third-party providers, the way many other companies had done in the past.

## *Learning Process*

Growing is always a learning process; gathering data and evaluating the processes are the main learning focuses. Pilot programs allow companies to have an idea about how markets and workflows behave.

With help and support from customers, the decision was made to target five senior couples with five sets of medical devices for them to do their vital signs measurements from home. This included devices like a blood pressure monitor, glucometers, pulse oximeter, scale, and temperature monitoring system.

A week later, all five kits were back at the office, and none of the couples wanted anything to do with vital sign collection. Little did we know that technology, without human touch and ease of use, does not help at all. From this, we learned that improvements in several areas were needed for the technology to work. Adjustments were made both on the technology and the human interaction (using wellness coaching techniques), resulting in many satisfied customers using the platform in earnest.

When the CMS came up with five Remote Patient Monitoring CPT Codes,[1] it opened a huge opportunity to improve patient care and enhance provider revenue. Billing for these codes would enable a Medical Provider who cares for Medicare patients to earn more than $170 using RPM.

## *Bright Future*

Esvyda has been dedicated to improving and refining the design, development, and marketing of software products for chronic disease management, Remote Patient Monitoring, and Behavioral Health Integration with a focus on diabetes, hypertension, and CHF. We also started experimenting with Artificial Intelligence, Big Data analytics, and with new cellular or IoT (Internet of Things) like wearable options and other devices that will have communication capabilities similar to a mobile phone. This will enable faster communication between doctors and patients.

# Why the Need for Remote Patient Monitoring (RPM)?

Remote Patient Monitoring enables physicians to access real-time data to prevent complications and significantly improve a patient's quality of life. In addition, patients and their family members feel comfortable knowing that they are being monitored and will be supported if any problems arise. RPM will also help avoid costly ER visits and needless hospitalizations through proactive intervention.

In this era of digitalization and consumerization in healthcare, healthcare providers need to be at the forefront of such digitalization if they want to be competitive. Although we know the human touch is important when caring for patients, we think digitalization in healthcare complements how doctors treat patients, and at the same time, it may attract more patients, mostly young. Nowadays, patients are empowered to make the best decisions about their health as new options are open to them.

# Challenges and Benefits for Remote Patient Monitoring (RPM)

## *For Providers/Clinicians*

One of the biggest challenges Health Providers have is a way to help patients see how remote patient monitoring really works and how the benefits far outweigh the costs of such a solution. The best way for Technology Providers to address these issues is to design a simple process for patients to follow with an easy-to-use solution, pointing them in the right direction to implement the best telehealth option, while ensuring very reasonable pricing for the software and devices.

## Guiding the Customers

Having a healthy relationship with the client is vital to any business in the healthcare industry. This relationship will grow stronger based on trust: listening to them carefully and understanding the solution that customers want to implement. Getting to know the client's specific needs, their exist-ing workflow, and the way they are planning to use the equipment, helps to suggest particular devices from which they can reap optimum benefits.

## The Human Touch

Complementing and enhancing physical care, empowering primary doctors, and caring for patients with a human touch is paramount. Digitalization in healthcare may complement how doctors treat patients and at the same time, it may attract more young patients. Online consultations may be a good option to give expert medical advice and help with follow-ups for treatments of almost all medical conditions.

This human presence is reflected in the interest in taking care of the patient in every way possible. A patient's environmental factors play a cru-cial role in the patient's treatment adherence and health outcomes. These may be addressed using online consultations and remote patient monitoring. Lifestyle, physical activity, and nutrition may be integrated to treat a patient in a holistic way; thus, patients may be treated anytime, anywhere.

## Pricing and Costs

Technology providers must commit to helping providers to provide afford-able healthcare services and cost savings to the healthcare system, while also helping patients to achieve better health outcomes by using comfortable telehealth options and Remote Patient Monitoring tools.

For instance, appointment cancellation may be avoidable because prob-lems relative to transportation may be solved. This is a good advantage for patients living by themselves with physical disabilities, as well as for elderly people or patients in rural areas.

No-shows cost the US healthcare system more than $150 billion USD a year, and for individual physicians, an average of $200 USD per unused time slot, negatively impacting revenue and patient care continuity. After all, whether patients show up or not, healthcare organizations and medical practices must still pay their staff and cover fixed expenses, like rent.[2,3]

## For Patients and Consumers

Remote patient monitoring of vital signs and physical activity solutions can improve and complement personalized treatments or the care provided by doctors to patients for disease prevention. Also, virtual care improves the patient-centric approach, because it provides other channels of communication such as secure messages, text messages (SMS), or emails between doctors, care teams, patients, and families.

## Mental and Sexual Health Diseases

These diseases are still considered taboo subjects in almost all cultures, so the rate of appointment cancellations represents a significant reduction in the income of doctors of these specialties. Telemedicine may be a more private option to address these issues because patients may feel more comfortable talking about these issues directly from their places and environments of their choice. These may be treated using telehealth and remote patient monitoring as individuals or in group therapy settings, as well as the involvement of their families.

## Medication Management

Appointments may be booked to follow up on prescriptions. That way, doctors may adjust regimens according to progress in treatment, patients' feedback, and medical history.

## Other Benefits

■ Readmission and Emergency Room visit reduction through follow-up video consultations, secure messages, remote monitoring of medical and mental health of patients.
■ The best options for post-discharge programs and short-, medium-, and long-term treatments for patients with chronic conditions.
■ Time flexibility for people who do not have enough time to spend in a waiting room because of their work schedule or other commitments. They can easily contact the doctor using online video consultations.

- For the management of women's healthcare programs, such as pregnancy, maternity, and infant care.
- Telehealth could be cheaper than a traditional office visit, therefore more affordable for patients.
- Doctors can check in with more patients per day or review them faster.
- For the treatment follow-up of minor injuries like:
  - Sprains and Strains.
  - Broken Bones.
  - Arm and leg injuries.
  - Cuts and grazes
  - Burns and scalds.
  - Eye injuries.
  - Minor head injuries.
  - Insect and animal bites.
  - Allergic reactions

## Comparative Analysis

### Benefits

The implementation of a Remote Patient Monitoring program is not a free result for institutions. It is evident that economic, human, technological, and time resources must be invested. This is with the aim of obtaining great benefits not only for the health of patients, but also to increase the income and revenue of healthcare providers.

RPM provides a wide range of benefits for practices with the objective of improving the population's health outcomes, and reducing patient, provider, and overall healthcare costs.

Some of the most relevant benefits of RPM are:

- Adding a previously untapped source of revenue: Value-based care rewards healthcare providers with incentives based on the quality of care they provide to patients. 90% of the nation's $3.8 trillion in annual health expenditures is for people with chronic and mental health conditions[4,5] patients who can be treated using remote monitoring strategies.
- Keeping people healthy: In the US, around 78% of people over 55 years old in the US are suffering from 1+ chronic conditions and 47% have

at least 2+ chronic conditions. Given such levels of disease, prevention programs play a vital role in efforts and strategies aimed at improving the long-term health of the population and reducing costs associated with disease treatment.

■ Reducing the number of hospitalizations: Monitoring patients in real time will allow healthcare providers to predict and anticipate higher-cost events. Prompt action can prevent illnesses before they become serious.

■ Reducing readmissions: Being admitted to a hospital again is not only uncomfortable for the patient, but is also a reprocessing that could be avoided by monitoring after the patient's discharge.

■ Reducing hospital length of stay: A constant and effective monitoring of the patient's health can mean a shorter stay in the hospital since after a few days the patient could be monitored from home.

■ Keeps patient's independence: RPM allows older and disabled individuals to remain at home longer, and delay or avoid moving into skilled nursing facilities.

■ Can also bill RPM as CCM

■ Can add Behavioral Health Integration to practice

■ The positive public relations image of the practice being up to par with new technology

## Investment

■ Transition time: The period it takes for the solution to be implemented, plus the time necessary to adapt the workflows and processes.

■ Cost: The money that is invested in the implementation of the solution, including time, personnel, and equipment. In addition to the subscription to the RPM service (monthly/per patient)

■ Training Staff: Learning to use a new platform means that staff will invest time in training processes, thus using the platform and tools in the most efficient way possible.

■ Patient qualification and selection: The time and effort invested in the process of verifying which patients are covered by insurers or can apply for RPM services

■ Determine the best platform and support: Since there are a wide variety of companies that provide remote monitoring services, healthcare providers should take the time to study the market and select the technology solution that best meets their needs.

An example: (Based on experience and market investigations)
A healthcare institution with an average of 1,150 remote monitored
   patients can bill for these services $1.8 million USD per year
Taking into account all the investment needed for running an RPM program, and a margin of 90% claims acceptance, a practice can make
   approximately $474,100 USD per year.
*Billed RPM Income − Investments / Costs = Revenue*

$$1,800,000\$-(aprox)1,326,000\$=474,000/\ year$$

The four main components of a successful RPM program are: Methodology,
Software Implementation, Devices, and Research and Development.

## Methodology/Flow

The adaptability of the RPM monitoring systems to quickly integrate and
intercommunicate with different stakeholders of the patient's healthcare
process puts the information in the palm of patients, care teams, EHRs,
healthcare institutions, and more. This connectivity network produces results
within seconds and alerts physicians and caregivers to an abnormal reading
through a simple text or email.

## Software Implementation

To ensure the patient's information security, strong encryption protocols
for the information process are needed from storage to transit and then to
delivery. None of the data in transit contains any electronic protected health
information (ePHI) until it reaches the telehealth system.

Versatility to connect with all stakeholders is due to the use of tools such
as APIs and SDKs. These allow a much faster, more stable, and more efficient connection.

## Devices (Medical and Wearables)

There are many ways to input patient-generated data into a cloud-based
platform where patients and care teams can use medical and wearable
devices. According to the customers' workflows and needs, devices can
connect via Bluetooth LE, cellular connectivity (using a SIM card), or
Gateways. Also, information can be entered manually via a mobile app
or web portal in case the patients or care teams have devices without the
option of wireless connection.

This provides doctors with the ability to see results in real time. For example, if they need to take care of a diabetic patient, RPM-enabled devices can measure the condition and show them the results in seconds. On the compliance side, a HIPAA-compliant system provides tools that empower healthcare professionals and caregivers to remotely monitor their patients' health conditions, add notes, and keep track of time spent performing patient activities.

RPM platforms can support various measurement data uploads, including blood glucose, blood pressure, temperature, blood oxygen, and weight. Patients' test results are sent via a cellular connection using a 4G Hub or mobile app to the cloud. If the results are abnormal or out-of-range, the doctor can take action by contacting the patient to prevent hospitalization.

## Research and Development

R&D is always important for coming up with new products that are simple, easy to use, and more efficient. This is one of the major factors that places healthcare technology companies ahead of the competition, this in addition to the quick response time to the clients' problems or questions.

## A Medical Group in Florida

A medical group in Florida was facing a major problem with the patients not being compliant with health plan compliance and some HIPAA regulations. The main reason for this was the group's inability to communicate with patients in an efficient, quick, and proper way.

A process where patients were handed a device that enabled them to measure their own condition efficiently was implemented. This was followed by a doctor obtaining the compliant data seamlessly, as everything was running through the device, the middleware, and the Esvyda cloud. Their compliance problem was solved.

## Happy Couple

A 52-year-old woman and a 54-year-old man with diabetes, hypertension, and obesity, who enrolled in the Telemonitoring Pilot Program from July 7 to September 22 in 2017, were actively engaged through Lifestyle Coaching.

## Patient engagement and care coordination

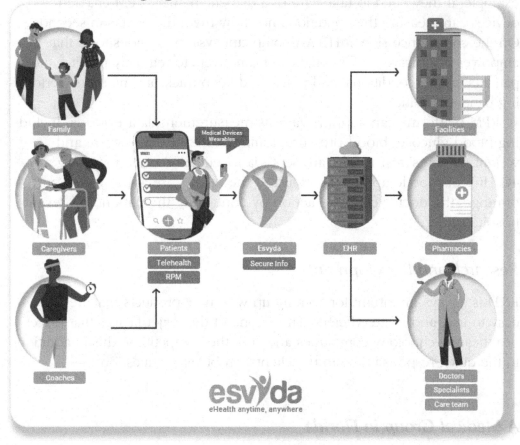

**Figure 6.1 Success Stories.**

Coaches motivated them daily to take readings and keep doctor's prescriptions, acting as "Partners," listening to them without "Judgment," and sharing similar experiences.

Neither readmission to the hospital nor ER visits happened. They were more self-conscious about their health and started using their garage as a small gym to work out every day, because they wanted to be an example for their grandchildren.

> I keep forgetting to mention that my husband & I converted 1/2 of our garage into a mini gym, no more excuses:)
> Things are going good, I have set a good example to my kids, and everyone is working out

## Mr. S.

A 75-year-old man with diabetes and hypertension enrolled in the Telemonitoring Pilot Program from June 2017 to date.

He has been followed up with by Lifestyle Coaches, who have been partners and listeners, and he has been keeping an eye on his readings.

When an episode of out-of-range blood pressure readings was shown on the platform, the Wellness Coach communicated with the doctor immediately and an appointment was set up to proactively intervene and possibly avoid any complications that might have sent the patient to the hospital.

The doctor raised the medication dosage, and the problem was resolved.

## Notes

1 CPT Codes: The Current Procedural Terminology codes describe the service provided by the healthcare professional. The RPM Codes associated with our services are 99091, 99453, 99454, 99457, and 99458
2 Gier J (2017): Missed appointments cost the U.S. healthcare system $150B each year. Available online at: www.scisolutions.com/uploads/news/Missed-Appts-Cost-HMT-Article-042617.pdf
3 Hayhurst C (2019): No-show effect: Even one missed appointment risks retention. Available online at: www.athenahealth.com/knowledge-hub/financial-performance/no-show-effect-even-one-missed-appointment-risks-retention
4 Buttorff C, Ruder T, Bauman M (2017): *Multiple Chronic Conditions in the United States*, Santa Monica, CA: Rand Corp.
5 Martin AB, Hartman M, Lassman D, Catlin A (2020). National health care spending in 2019: Steady growth for the fourth consecutive year. *Health Aff.* 40(1):1–11.

## Chapter 7

# RPM Data to Enable Improved Patient Care (Who Uses RPM Data?)

Michael W. Davis

## Contents

## Getting Timely and Accurate RPM Data to Drive Expected Outcomes

COVID-19, the movement of US healthcare to value-based reimbursement, and population health models have highlighted the need to provider better monitoring of high-risk patients to deliver expected healthcare outcomes. Remote patient monitoring (RPM) provides the ability to capture real-time patient data that allows providers to have a more accurate view of the patient's healthcare status. Patient care is frequently disjointed as patients move between care modalities. Providers have acquired and merged with

DOI: 10.4324/9781003304036-8

other provider organizations to create networks of care services that are needed to support patients in various clinical states. The reality of patient care is that patients do not stay within the provider networks, especially when specialty care may be needed (e.g., surgery, endocrinology, immunology, cancer care, cardiac care). Patients who receive care within and outside of a provider network create challenges for the clinicians who are next in line to treat them. RPM data that is captured but not presented to physicians at each care encounter elevates the risk to the patient's care.

Diabetic and cardiology patients represent RPM examples where data captured over a period of time will be invaluable, preventing emergency department visits or re-admissions/admissions to acute care hospitals. Preventing these events results in higher-quality and profitable population health programs.

The challenge is how to close the loop for distributing the most recent RPM data to the provider who is now seeing the patient to render care and using the data within the provider EHR for diagnostic result trending and clinical decision support.

## RPM Device and EHR Interoperability

The first step in closing the patient care loop is to integrate RPM data into the EHR workflows that support physician inboxes, trending of RPM data, and clinical decision support (CDS) interactions. Only relevant RPM data should be sent to physician inboxes in order to reduce physician burnout. The ability to trend RPM data that can be displayed with other diagnostic data will allow physicians to evaluate the current health status of a patient to determine whether the patient is improving or declining. The ability to use RPM data with CDS systems based on artificial intelligence (AI) will generate useful alerts for clinicians to guide patient interventions based on evidence-based medicine protocols.

## RPM and Telehealth/Telemedicine Integration

Telehealth/telemedicine programs exploded during the pandemic. The ability to provide remote/virtual care to patients protected both the patients and care providers during the care delivery process and has resulted in the FDA issuing guidance for expanding non-invasive RPM device use. Several providers in various states across the US have implemented RPM with their telehealth/telemedicine programs. All these programs have been established to monitor patients with chronic diseases that represent higher expense and risk groups in population health programs.

It must be noted that RPM integration in telehealth/telemedicine services must translate to data feeds that also support the EHR receiving the RPM data used in the telehealth/telemedicine service. The provider care delivery environments must create effective data interoperability between RPM devices, telehealth/telemedicine, and EHR environments. A key success factor for this capability will be the adoption of the CMS interoperability regulations based on HL7 FHIR API data sharing services.

Health information exchanges (HIEs) should be provided RPM data from connected EHR environments. Again, RPM data is extremely valuable for understanding shifts in patient health status that can assist clinicians with establishing effective care plans and additional RPM services when needed.

Providers may also share the RPM data with emerging large-technology company data warehouse and analytics environments that will be used to support AI programs and to drive improved evidence-based medicine protocols. Examples are the Google Cloud Healthcare Data Engine and the Amazon Health Lake.

# RPM Expectations

Timely and relevant RPM data can provide advantages to providers in the following areas:

- Reduced ED visits. RPM data that can be monitored for abnormal results that generate care alerts may allow providers to adjust medications and patient activities that prevent an ED visit. Again, this is important for providers who are taking on risk contracts for managing the health of patient populations.
- 30-day re-admission preventions. RPM data may identify early patient clinical indicators that can be used to generate virtual care interventions to prevent the patient from being re-admitted to the hospital within 30 days of discharge for the same health issue(s). These re-admission costs are borne by the hospital for risk contracts and can be very expensive.
- Improved medication compliance. The ability to monitor patient vital signs and diagnostic data will likely permit the providers to recognize

if patients are compliant with taking their medications as prescribed, or if the dosages or routes need to be modified. Even if patients are filling their prescriptions, it does not mean they are taking the medications as prescribed.

■ Improved support of home care or acute care at home services. The pandemic highlighted the need to deliver patient-focused healthcare to modalities of care that best fit the needs of the patient. As RPM technologies become more advanced, the ability to integrate RPM data with patient engagement/communication services will enable home care clinicians to support patients more effectively with services that are delivered to the patient's home. This reduces patient risk for traveling to receive care, exposure to infections at clinics or the hospital, and supports better mental health for the patients.

■ Supporting care equity. Many minorities receive infrequent and disjointed care services due to access issues. Several states cover RPM services for their Medicaid patients. Providing RPM services for high-risk Medicaid patients with chronic diseases will reduce state costs for these programs.

## Market Drivers

1. Standardization of RPM outputs. Groups such as Continua strive to develop standards for adoption by medical device vendors that will enable efficient data interoperability exchanges between the devices and clinical application environments (e.g., EHR and telehealth/telemedicine products). The success of standards groups for normalizing RPM data will be a critical success factor lowering RPM device and integration costs.

2. Interoperability standards adoption by EHR and telehealth/telemedicine vendors. As stated previously in this chapter, the adoption by the healthcare IT vendor industry of the CMS interoperability standards will enable better RPM data sharing across modalities of care and clinical care applications.

3. Continued emergence of smartphones as a highly adopted RPM device. Smartphones are emerging as key RPM devices that capture vital signs and voice biomarkers that can provide early disease detection. Smartphones are ubiquitous across all socio-economic categories in the US. Smartphones will enable more effective, efficient, and lower-cost

healthcare services in the US. In areas where there is no internet and/or WiFi service, lower-cost 3G cell phone services will suffice for exchanging RPM data. Smartphones are becoming the obvious future "wearables" of choice for RPM.

## Summary

Both patients and providers benefit from RPM services and resulting timely data that can be shared between the patients and multiple providers to manage care and communicate care guidance more effectively. RPM data can help close the loop for knowing the status of high-risk patients and potential care interventions that may be needed to bring the patient into compliance with evidence-based medicine protocols that improve outcomes, care quality, and patient satisfaction.

To deliver on the potential benefits of RPM data, the RPM devices must integrate with EHR and telehealth/telemedicine applications for real-time sharing of data. The RPM data should be integrated into EHR and telehealth/telemedicine application workflows to take advantage of clinical decision support functions that can generate actionable alerts to clinicians that will improve patient care and safety.

While disease-specific RPM solutions will continue to provide value for controlling the cost and quality of care for high-risk patients with chronic diseases, devices that can monitor several patient clinical attributes will become more valuable for providers trying to control acquisition, maintenance, replacement, and integration costs. Over time, smartphones are likely to become the multifactorial RPM devices of choice for providers.

# STANDARDS AND REGULATORY

**2**

# Chapter 8

# Regulatory and Emerging Standards

Michael W. Davis

## Contents

## Connected Home Over IP May Drive Improved Home Care

### The Problem: Emerging Digital Appliances Often Lack Standards for Interoperability

Many emerging technology environments end up with disjointed capabilities for connections with IT environments or with other devices. This results in tremendous waste for consumers, as these solutions may be more prone to technical obsolescence as well as replacement costs. In many cases, the rush to get a digital appliance to market with a minimum viable market design

DOI: 10.4324/9781003304036-10

results in early versions of solutions that may not support future user needs or the ability to create appropriate technology or data connections with other digital solutions. In these environments, standards are often a follow-on process that are driven by consumer demand and need.

A great example of this was the early launch of digital glucometers on the market over a decade ago. The Continua Health Alliance[25] was formed from several glucometer vendors to create a standard for these devices to share data with IT environments.

COVID-19 has become the catalyst for driving higher levels of digital technology adoption to support telehealth/telemedicine and home care. As healthcare moves to create an interoperable environment via CMS regulations[26], the US healthcare system is transforming into a data-driven environment that is needed to reduce costs and improve care quality. Consumers will expect their digital healthcare devices to easily connect and share data with their providers directly or via their smart home systems. These challenges will be significantly reduced for smart home solutions with an emerging standard.

## The Solution: Smart Home Standards That Will Improve RPM

Apple, Google, Amazon, and Zigbee are joining together to launch a new standard for developing digital appliances that interact with their smart home solutions. This new standard is called Connected Home Over IP (CHIP)[27]. Apple has open-sourced some components of its HomeKit Accessory Development Kit (ADK) to help expedite the development of digital accessory products with this standard. Google is promoting this standard to also include digital applications on mobile phones and for interactions with cloud environments. Google believes this standard with IP will eliminate the need for routers and wired networks that complicate the smart home environments today. Bluetooth Low Energy protocols and Thread (IEEE 802.15.4 network protocol) will likely become more established for communications with accessory devices for the smart home solutions.

Smart home standards for connecting accessories will help reduce the risk for consumers in purchasing digital remote monitoring devices that will improve healthcare protocol compliance, remote patient monitoring (RPM), and the ability to share their medical data more easily and securely with their providers.

Currently, smart home solutions are acquired by the middle and higher economic classes of citizens. But, as these environments evolve to also become the gateways for streaming services, they could replace the cable boxes that exist for most economic classes in this country. Conversely, the cable companies could evolve their services to become smart home solutions. The ability to provide real-time medical monitoring of consumers in their home environments will provide a significant advancement for healthcare access and quality.

## The Justification: Alexa Says, "Time for Your Medicine"

Smart home solutions are becoming personal assistants for consumers to support their daily activities. The ability to add healthcare functions to these environments will establish a new remote patient monitoring capability that can also be complemented with medical content to support patient compliance with their current therapies. The smart home solutions could be linked to CHIP-compliant medical devices and wearables that would automatically capture and transmit patient data to providers that will likely improve chronic disease outcomes. These solutions could also monitor patient compliance with their medication accessories (e.g., digital pill containers) or exercise devices connected via CHIP. Alexa could become a medical nag!

## The Players: Smart Home Device Companies

Smart home solution companies will continue to expand consumer services via standards for connecting digital accessories. Representative companies include:

- Apple Home app: an iOS environment that connects applications and devices compliant with Apple's HomeKit framework.
- Google Nest: the Google Android smart home assistant solution.
- Amazon Echo: the Amazon smart home solution that includes Alexa as the smart assistant.

## Success Factors

- Healthcare organizations that plan to connect to patients via smart home solutions now need to ensure that the medical accessories used are CHIP-compliant.
- Smart home connections with providers should be approached with a prototype mentality to thoroughly test out the capabilities for using these environments to extend patient care effectively and safely.
- Successful interoperability by providers with smart home solutions should be heavily marketed to drive competitive advantage.

## Summary

The smart home environment is well positioned to help providers extend their patient care services and remote patient monitoring capabilities. COVID-19 has created a "woke" environment for patient-focused care globally. Home care will continue to grow as a significant healthcare delivery service that will improve patient satisfaction, reduce healthcare costs, and increase patient safety and expected outcomes.

As large technology companies such as Amazon, Apple, and Google continue to focus their digital solutions and cloud environments to support new digital healthcare solutions, the rate of adoption of these solutions by consumers will continue to grow. Healthcare organizations that are patient-focused will begin to establish medical data sharing services with smart home solutions to create a new channel for effectively engaging patients in their care. As smart home solutions continue to expand their healthcare support capabilities and services, they may be well positioned to become the personal health record environment for their customers.

"Every once in a while, a new technology, an old problem, and a big idea turn into an innovation."—Dean Kamen

# Chapter 9

# Payment Strategies and Codes

Michael W. Davis

## Contents

COVID-19 has expedited the need to use remote patient monitoring (RPM) services to better manage a patient's care, while also protecting the patient and providers from potential infections that may occur with face-to-face visits. Common Procedural Terminology 4th Edition (CPT4) codes have been expanded to provide a higher level of service definition for using RPM and are expanding with the addition of remote therapy monitoring (RTM) codes. The American Telemedicine Association (ATA) is asking for improved service relationships between RPM and RTP codes and also adding "G"codes. The ATA writes:

> These G codes will allow for incident-to billing and are essential to ensuring auxiliary personnel and clinical staff are able to assist in the provision of RTM services under the general supervision of a billing provider, as correctly questioned by CMS.

DOI: 10.4324/9781003304036-11

## Current CPT4 RPM Codes

Current CPT4 codes used by physicians for RPM services as described by the Prevounce Blog consists of:

**CPT 99453** (single payment from Medicare of about $21)

The description of CPT 99453 is: "Remote monitoring of physiologic parameter(s) (e.g., weight, blood pressure, pulse oximetry, respiratory flow rate), initial; set-up and patient education on use of equipment."

**CPT 99454** (monthly payment from Medicare around $64 for a practice)

The description of CPT 99454 is: "Remote monitoring of physiologic parameter(s) (e.g., weight, blood pressure, pulse oximetry, respiratory flow rate), initial; device(s) supply with daily recording(s) or programmed alert(s) transmission, each 30 days."

**CPT 99457** (20 minutes of care management services, covered by Medicare, averages a payment of $55; if a "minimum" amount of services is provided to 50 patients, a practice will receive about $72,000 in Medicare reimbursement every 12 months.)

The description of CPT 99457 is: "Remote physiologic monitoring treatment management services, clinical staff/physician/other qualified health care professional time in a calendar month requiring interactive communication with the patient/caregiver during the month; initial 20 minutes."

**CPT 99458** (for patients who require more than 20 minutes of care management services during an RPM session; averages a payment of $44 to cover an additional 20 minutes of care management services; practices cannot bill more than 60 minutes of care management services per month.)

The description of CPT 99458 is: "Remote physiologic monitoring treatment management services, clinical staff/physician/other qualified health care professional time in a calendar month requiring interactive communication with the patient/caregiver during the month; additional 20 minutes."

### CPT 99091

We stated that there were four essential RPM CPT codes, which are identified here. There is a fifth CPT code that's worth knowing about because it's a code **you likely want to avoid: CPT 99091**. This was the initial code that practices used to bill for remote patient monitoring. While CPT 99091 is still accepted by CMS when billing for remote patient monitoring in 2020, it is no longer advisable to do so since the aforementioned RPM codes represent better options for the vast majority of situations.

## RTM Proposed Codes

Building off of guidelines set by the American Medical Association's Digital Medicine Payment Advisory Group over the past year, CMS has proposed the following CPT codes for RTM coverage in 2022:

**CPT code 989X1**: Remote therapeutic monitoring (e.g., respiratory system status, musculoskeletal system status, therapy adherence, therapy response), initial set-up and patient education on use of equipment;

**CPT code 989X2**: Remote therapeutic monitoring (e.g., respiratory system status, musculoskeletal system status, therapy adherence, therapy response), device(s) supply with scheduled (e.g., daily) recording(s) and/or programmed alert(s) transmission to monitor respiratory system, each 30 days;

**CPT code 989X3**: Remote therapeutic monitoring (e.g., respiratory system status, musculoskeletal system status, therapy adherence, therapy response), device(s) supply with scheduled (e.g., daily) recording(s) and/or programmed alert(s) transmission to monitor musculoskeletal system, each 30 days;

**CPT code 989X4**: Remote therapeutic monitoring treatment management services, physician/other qualified health care professional time in a calendar month requiring at least one interactive communication with the patient/caregiver during the calendar month; first 20 minutes; and

**CPT code 989X5**: Remote therapeutic monitoring treatment management services, physician/other qualified healthcare professional time in a calendar month requiring at least one interactive communication with the patient/caregiver during the calendar month, each additional 20 minutes (list separately in addition to code for primary procedure).

**CMS is proposing to reimburse RTM service codes 989X4 and 989X5 at the same rate as it reimburses for RPM services in codes 99457 and 99458**.

## Reimbursements for RPM and RTM Will Drive Quick Adoption by Providers

The best way to drive adoption of technologies and services by US providers is by reimbursing them for their time and effort. The pandemic and patient-focused care will drive providers to more quickly adopt remote patient monitoring technologies to improve care quality and patient satisfaction. Value-based care reimbursement will also expedite the use of remote patient monitoring solutions that improve the providers ability to manage population health at-risk contracts.

A side benefit of RPM and RTM for providers is the addition of patient data that can be used to further improve AI-based clinical decision support and business/clinical analytics to drive higher levels of patient safety and care quality. The use of this data will become more prevalent as RPM and RTM solutions become interoperable with the provider EHR systems.

# Chapter 10

# Medical-Grade Interoperability

Michael J. Kirwan

## Contents

Remote monitoring encompasses capturing and securing data in dynamic mobile environments outside of the clinical environment: such as the tracking, storing and forwarding of a person's vital signs data and their measurement timestamps as they travel over different time zones, in environments with no connectivity and in instances of an abrupt loss of connectivity or power. This includes protecting and securing the person's privacy while ensuring responsiveness of concerns encountered during the monitoring of their data.

Achieving medical-grade interoperability means that multiple sensor types of data, e.g., vital sign sensor data from a glucose monitor, a blood pressure cuff, a pulse-oximeter, thermometer or any other CDG remote monitoring device, may be sent separately or combined as multi-measurements and be clearly understood by healthcare providers end-to-end—all the while the context of the data remains. This offers healthcare providers an authentic and holistic view and understanding of the data because the chemical, biological and medical science data is understood through its comprehensive nomenclature coding system. Medical-grade interoperability can only be achieved through harmonization with existing adopted healthcare standards and protocols understood by regulatory agencies, governments, EHRs, clinicians, etc. and as validated with the muster and rigor of a globally accepted conformity acceptance scheme requiring the very best practices for compliance and interoperability. Therefore, medical-grade interoperability is only validated by demonstrating compliance with both the IEEE 11073 Personal Health Device specifications (protocols and specializations for health, medical and fitness remote monitoring) and the CDG through the Continua certification process.

PCHAlliance believes that any organization interested in being part of the health IoT ecosystem should be able to achieve medical-grade interoperability and claim compliance to the CDG. To make this possible, PCHAlliance provides both the CDG and its automated Continua test tool freely to any organization. Membership within the PCHAlliance is also inexpensive for organizations to join and certify. And, if they certify, the PCHAlliance will help organizations match buyers to sellers through its Continua Certified Product Showcase and social media channels. If not ready to join and certify, the PCHAlliance will post on its web site the organization's self-declaration of Continua compliance. Also, to help organizations expedite their development of medical-grade interoperability, PCHAlliance is developing Continua's Open Development Environment (CODE) for Healthcare project, which creates commercial-ready software to accelerate commercial adoption of products that employ the Continua devices and services interfaces. CODE for Healthcare is developed in accordance with ISO 62304, which will help streamline regulatory approvals and will help simplify ubiquitous secure delivery of Continua device data into health systems.

## Scaling for the Internet of Healthy Interoperability

The situation today is that few IoT organizations know the value or potential that the CDG can provide for IoT. Few organizations are thinking of a globally interoperable network, which is why proprietary networks have pervaded, but so far have failed to unlock even a slice of what the CDG can offer—which is big data research, analytics and authentic medical-grade interoperability.

Large-scale IoT connectivity for healthcare through the use of Continua's open data model is considered a requisite for many newer technologies such as virtual reality, augmented reality, artificial intelligence, smart cities, autonomous vehicles, etc. Continua's open data model can also work with IoT transport technologies such as 5G, NB-IoT, LTE-M, LoRa and CAT-M1 and others. The scalability of IoT solutions for healthcare is possible through medical-grade interoperability, utilizing the data model approved by stakeholders worldwide and as specified by the CDG. Big data research is not possible through the proprietary API walled-garden approach where only a few organizations can participate or share the data. Organizations attempting to scale by integrating the many different approaches for data can more likely succeed in the long run if they implement to the CDG. Clear, transparent and interoperable data is the objective, as it helps the approvers and consumers of the data trust, believe and accept what is meaningful and holistic—which leads to better health outcomes.

Of passive sensors, the smartphone is the most ubiquitous. It has a nine-axis inertial motion sensor that tracks motion and position in three-dimensional space. A three-axis accelerometer measures acceleration in the x, y, and z axes; a three-axis gyroscope senses rotation around each axis; and a three-axis magnetometer compensates for magnetic drift to maintain position accuracy. These sensors enable physics-based capabilities, such as detecting the number of steps that a person takes during a day. Most smartphones can also sense geographic position, atmospheric pressure, ambient light, voice, and touchscreen pressure. Creative uses of these sensors and a built-in camera can turn the smartphone into a fall detector, a spirometer (by sensing air pressure on the microphone) or a heart-rate sensor.

Wearable devices are also widespread. In the United States in 2017, 17% of adults used a wearable device such as a smartwatch or a wrist-worn fitness band. Wrist sensors have many of the same sensors as smartphones and can be used to detect motions such as those associated with smoking.

# COMPONENTS OF WEARABLE DEVICES

3

# Chapter 11

# Physiological Sensors

Walter N. Maclay

## Contents

DOI: 10.4324/9781003304036-14

# Use Cases in Health Care

## Glucose Monitoring

There are now patches that monitor glucose continuously. They are called Continuous Glucose Monitors, or CGM. They are small enough to not interfere with daily activities, and they can be worn in the shower. These devices are more comfortable and less intrusive than collecting blood from the finger several times a day. Many young people are uncomfortable having their friends see them doing a glucose test, because it makes them seem different. This makes a CGM device attractive. In the future, calibration may not be required, making it even more convenient. They have a single needle that penetrates the skin to sample blood, although they are comfortable and can be worn up to two weeks. It is necessary to calibrate the device when it is first installed. The patient pricks a finger and gets a reading with a standard glucose measurement device which is entered into the CGM device, typically using a smartphone. Two leading players in this market are Abbott Diabetes and Dexcom.

There is a glucose monitor that fits into the eye. It has appeared in many reports, but it is only a laboratory study device. It has not been made into a commercial device. The accuracy has not been reported. It is unlikely that it meets FDA requirements for accuracy.

## Insulin Pumps

Wearable insulin pumps have existed for many years. People in the diabetes community have nefariously hacked them to integrate with continuous glucose monitors, creating a complete closed loop wearable pancreas replacement. Notably, manufacturers of insulin pumps and continuous glucose monitors have reduced their efforts to make their devices resistant to hacking. There seems to be an acceptance by these companies and the FDA that it is ok for hackers to create their own devices, as long as they don't sell them. There is now a closed loop system that uses a CGM device from one company and an insulin pump from another. This is a novel example of the FDA approving a combination of two devices from two different companies. See Chapter 1 for further information.

## Chest Patches for Cardiac Monitoring

In recent years, several companies have developed patches that adhere to the chest for cardiac monitoring. The patches can be worn for a week at a time, even in the shower. This gives a more complete picture of a person's cardiac condition, particularly for events that don't happen regularly, such as atrial fibrillation. They can collect and transmit data wirelessly. They are replacing Holter monitors for collection of cardiac data, because they are more convenient, lower-cost, and they can provide several days of data. It is common to send data wirelessly, allowing these devices to be used for real-time monitoring. What is holding back adoption is the lack of artificial intelligence software to monitor the data and detect anomalies that should be reviewed by healthcare professionals. With continuous monitoring, there is more data collected than anyone can effectively review. This limits the usefulness for real-time monitoring.

Cardiac monitors record ECG, but they may also monitor respiration, temperature, and blood oxygen.

## Watches for Cardiac Monitoring

According to HealthTech Magazine*, smartwatches are now helping healthcare providers collect and analyze a wider swath of data from patients between their appointments or after surgery. This data provides crucial and very valuable insights that can help identify possible and proper treatment.

[*https://healthtechmagazine.net/article/2020/01/smartwatch-where-will-it-go-2020]

The smartwatch trend, which is continuously growing sales every year, has inspired organizations such as Ochsner Health System in New Orleans. In 2015, Ochsner launched a pioneer program to better track uncontrolled hypertension among its patients. Stanford University's study in 2019 revealed that the Apple Watch could identify heart rhythm irregularities, such as atrial fibrillation, a leading stroke risk, which can be detected with 84 percent accuracy. And to utilize this innovation, Ochsner now also utilizes the Apple Watch, which has benefited the doctors. The smart wearable device will send alerts about a patient's declining condition and send data to the healthcare in-charge's wrist, even if they are wearing gloves.

Samsung Electronics Co. Ltd launched the Galaxy Watch 3 in August 2020. The Galaxy Watch3 features a PPG sensor to monitor SpO2 levels. Also, with its enhanced accelerometer, the Watch3 smartwatch automatically detects hard falls. This smartwatch also records REM cycles, deep sleep, and total sleep time to score and help improve the quality of sleep.

These sensors are becoming popular in other wearable devices. Although watches are intended for personal health and not as medical devices, the Apple Watch did get FDA approval for detecting atrial fibrillation.

## Implanted Cardiac Monitors

Implanted devices are a separate class of wearable device. They require a medical procedure to install them, but they can provide better data, because they can be placed where they work best. Implanted pacemakers and defibrillators have existed for many years. More recently, tiny cardiac monitors have been developed. Medtronic makes the Reveal LINQ. It is only 1.2 cubic centimeters in volume, and its battery lasts for three years. At that time, it needs to be removed. It has a Bluetooth wireless connection. It is intended to monitor patients for various heart conditions that do not show symptoms for long periods of time. For many disease states, however, an external monitor can be used, reducing the invasive risk and cost.

## In-Hospital Monitoring

Instead of having a nurse collect vital health data, hospitals are beginning to use a patch that is applied when the patient checks in. The patches can collect data much more often and at lower cost. The data can be sent wirelessly to the patient health record. These monitors can measure temperature, heart rate, ECG, breathing rate, blood oxygen, and blood pressure. As is described here, blood pressure measurement without a cuff is only just becoming available, so it is currently not generally used for patient monitoring. There is work being done to have artificial intelligence (AI) software evaluate the data and predict adverse events, sending help to the person hours before the event can happen.

## Sleep Monitors

Sleep monitoring is a rapidly growing area for wearable devices. There are many consumer products that monitor sleep, but there are also medical devices. A medical sleep monitor is typically a patch that adheres to the abdomen. Wearable devices can monitor sleep better than going to a sleep lab, as it may be difficult for a person to sleep normally in an unusual environment. Wearable patches are normally wireless, so the person's movement is unconstrained. A wearable sleep monitor can be worn for several nights and collect more complete sleep information compared to one night at a sleep lab, and the cost is lower than a sleep lab. They typically monitor ECG, breathing rate, SpO2, motion, and temperature. Sometimes skin impedance, also called galvanic skin response or GSR, is also measured.

## Hearables

There has been development recently around hearables—devices in the ear for health monitoring. The ear is an excellent location for detecting heart rate, SpO2, and motion. With millions of people already wearing earbuds to listen to music, it seems natural to add sensors to the ear buds. This has not taken off, perhaps because the elderly who most need medical attention are less likely to want to use earbuds, or they have conflicts with their hearing aid devices.

## Stimulation to Treat Disease or Pain

TENS, or Transcutaneous Electrical Nerve Stimulation, has been used for years to treat pain, such as back pain. An electrical signal is applied between two electrodes. Certain frequencies have been found to have therapeutic value.

More recently, other wearable stimulation devices have appeared. There are devices that are implanted in the spine with an external control to treat intractable pain. This has become a major medical device area with several large competitors.

There is now a device worn on the wrist that treats essential tremors. Made by Cala Health, the device is turned on and provides stimulation that is noticeable but not painful for approximately 45 minutes. Relief is said to last for many hours after treatment.

## EEG Monitoring

EEG monitoring has been changing. New devices are getting useful information without a large number of leads placed all over the head and requiring shaving of hair. Ceribell makes a head band for monitoring the brain during a seizure. It has 10 electrodes around the band. No hair needs to be shaved. The EEG data is run through an algorithm to identify if the patient is having a seizure.

## *Magnetic Field Devices for Migraines*

Magnetic fields are being used to stop or reduce migraines with a device that mounts on the head. Due to the power consumption, these devices may need to plug into power or use large batteries, so they may not be considered wearable devices.

## *Augmented Reality and Virtual Reality Glasses*

Augmented reality glasses allow you to see your surroundings. The added content appears in front of the real world. You can get instructions or access patient records without touching anything. When fully implemented, this could really help in surgery and ER wards.

Virtual reality glasses display an entirely virtual world, and the wearer does not see the real world at all. This is primarily useful for training, where you may have a virtual hospital and virtual patients. A computer can control the pace of learning.

Training of healthcare professionals is becoming more important as technology keeps changing the way they perform their jobs. Some training is best done without a live patient. Other training requires a live patient. Both training approaches are benefiting from the use of augmented reality glasses and virtual reality glasses.

# Physiological Sensors Used in Wearable Devices

## *Body Temperature Measurement*

Temperature sensors are low-cost and there are many types available. However, measuring core body temperature, which is usually desired, is not simple. Skin temperature is often lower than the core body temperature, especially at the extremities. Many wearable devices are on the wrist, which is not a good place to take this measurement. The forehead, under the arms, and in the ears are good places, but most wearable devices are located elsewhere.

Hearables, wearable devices in the ears, now exist. Many people wear earbuds for long periods to listen to music. Sensors can be placed in these devices without making them much bigger. Besides temperature, the ear is a good place to measure heart rate and blood oxygen saturation.

Software can combine data from multiple sensors, "sensor fusion", to determine when skin temperature is likely to be near the core body temperature. If the skin is wet, the person may be perspiring or in a shower. In either case the skin temperature is not a good indicator of core body temperature. If the person has been outside in cold weather, the skin is likely to be cold. If the room temperature is moderate and the person has been moderately active, the skin is likely to be close to the core body temperature.

Wet skin is likely to be colder than the core body temperature. Moisture on the skin can be measured using galvanic skin response or GSR. The electrical impedance of the skin is measured with electrodes. The ambient temperature can be measured with a temperature sensor that is kept away from the skin. Activity can be measured with a motion sensor. These sensors can be integrated with software to produce sensor fusion.

## Motion Measurement

Motion of the body has been measured for decades. Step counters were originally mechanical devices used to estimate the distance walked or run. Now, low-cost motion sensors have replaced the mechanical devices. They are very small and consume very little battery power, so they are used in many devices as auxiliary sensors, sometimes for sensor fusion.

Step counting is a good measure of activity and is used in many consumer devices. The manufacturers of the motion sensors have developed advanced software that is able to measure step counts when mounted on the wrist or other places on the body. This is quite a feat, although it is not perfectly accurate. The software can work with the motion sensor on the wrist, ankle, or torso. The software algorithms are even able to determine with reasonable accuracy that a person is walking, standing, or sitting.

Motion sensors are also used to measure motion during sleep. With software interpreting the data, it is possible to measure the stage of sleep with good accuracy. This is important for sleep analysis, as well as for consumer products.

Motion sensors can measure gait, which can be used to indicate several conditions, such as dementia and Parkinson's Disease. The specificity of the indication is only moderate, but it is good enough to refer people for further diagnosis by a healthcare professional.

Another use is for dead reckoning—tracking someone's motion. Motion sensors are only accurate for a few minutes. They accumulate errors over time, but because of their low power they can be used as a substitute for

GPS, which is moderately power-hungry. The GPS can be turned on only every few minutes to save battery power, and the motion sensor can track the position while the GPS is off.

## Heart Rate Measurement

There are several ways to measure heart rate. ECG electrodes may be used. Two electrodes located on most parts of the body can pick up a good enough signal to measure heart rate, even where the signal is not sufficient for an ECG measurement. A pulse plethysmograph (PPG) sensor can be used to measure heart rate. It was originally used to measure blood oxygen, but the heart rate is a stronger signal that needs to be removed to sense oxygen. These sensors work quite well, even on the wrist.

It is also possible, but infrequently done, to measure heart rate with a pressure sensor located over an artery. The pressure pulse can be sensed just as a person can feel the heart rate by placing fingers on the inside of the wrist.

For either an ECG electrode or a PPG sensor, it is important that there be good contact with the skin. On a wrist device this may be uncomfortable, presenting a design challenge. In many cases heart rate is not needed continuously, and software can determine when the signal is good. When it is not good, the heart rate can be ignored.

## Blood Oxygen Measurement

Oxygen saturation or SpO2 is only measured with a pulse plethysmograph (PPG) sensor. A pulse oximeter uses a PPG sensor. Originally, they were clipped onto a finger. Light of at least two wavelengths is passed through the finger. Both wavelengths are sensitive to the pulse. One wavelength is absorbed by hemoglobin. One signal is subtracted from the signal of the other wavelength to remove the pulse. The result is an accurate measurement of SpO2. This is a transmissive pulse oximeter where the light passes through the body.

The transmissive PPG measurement is only possible on the finger or ear, where light can pass through. For other locations, a reflective PPG measurement is used. The measurement uses similar wavelengths of light and subtracts the pulse from the signal. The reflected signal is much weaker than the transmitted signal, so the measurement is more difficult. More signal processing is required. It does not work where the body does not have good blood perfusion, but good results have been achieved on the wrist.

## ECG, EEG, and EMG Measurement

All of these signals are voltages generated by the body. The sensor consists of electrodes to pick up the voltage and an amplifier to measure the tiny signal.

ECG (electrocardiogram) has been measured for a long time with laboratory equipment that typically uses 12 leads and wires to the equipment. Signal processing has improved to the point that single lead ECG measurements are almost as good as 12-lead measurements. Wearable devices almost always use two contacts (which is called single lead). The contacts are usually dry for convenience, although it is easier to get a good signal with wet electrodes. The contacts need to be spaced at least four cm apart to get a good signal. ECG cannot be measured on the legs or arms. On the head it would be obscured by the EEG signal. Successful measurements have been made in pants, where the electrodes are on the lower abdomen. There are implanted ECG monitors, but they are not as widely used as non-invasive wearable devices.

EEG (electroencephalogram) has been measured with electrodes placed on shaved areas of the scalp with wires to the equipment. Many non-critical EEG applications, such as for consumer products, use only two electrodes. The electrodes can be on the temples where the electrodes may be attached to glasses or a headband. Successful measurements have been made with a helmet that has electrodes at the end of projectiles that reach the scalp without shaving any hair. This is critical, as a wearable device that requires preparation, such as shaving, is inconvenient. The measurement can only be done on the head. The signal elsewhere is too small.

EMG (electromyogram) is the measurement of the signal that activates muscles. It is not a common medical test. It can be used to sense what muscles are moving, or in the case of people with stroke, the muscles that the brain has directed to move, even if they did not move. The electrodes need to be carefully placed. On the forearm, for example, you can sense the individual muscles moving the fingers, but they are only a few millimeters apart, and the arm does not have a good reference for accurately positioning electrodes.

## Respiration Rate Measurement

The number of breaths per minute can be measured with several techniques. An old and still viable way is with a chest strap. A sensor measures the change in length of the flexible strap as the chest moves. This is fine for a shirt with sensors. Most wearable devices are small or not located on the chest, and this technique is not suitable in those cases.

A nasal cannula can be used in a hospital. It is not convenient or comfortable for a wearable device.

Thoracic impedance is an accurate technique. The electrical impedance of the chest varies as the chest expands and contracts. A sensor like the GSR sensor measures the impedance. It is important to measure deep in the tissue and not the skin at the surface, so that changes in skin conductivity do not interfere. This sensor works well on the chest, but it has not worked on the wrist, although efforts have been made on this. The arm, being narrower than the chest, has a much higher impedance. Thus, the overall impedance is dominated by the arm, and the signal is too small to measure accurately.

Respiration rate can also be measured directly from the ECG signal after filtering out the heart rate. If the breathing rate is well below the heart rate, this can work, as the heart is affected by the movement of the chest during breathing.

## Blood Pressure Measurement

Up until 2021, the only way to get medically accurate blood pressure measurements without calibration on each person was with a cuff. This has changed. It is now possible to do this with at least two technologies.

A PPG sensor with advanced software can measure blood pressure. This was a big challenge, partly because the measurement is sensitive to skin color and motion. The different wavelengths of light pass through the skin differently. A clinical study was done by Valencell, Inc, that achieved medically accurate blood pressure measurement without calibration*. Now a small wearable device can measure blood pressure. The study used a sensor on the finger. They are working to achieve this result on other parts of the body.

[*https://valencell.com/featured/valencells-cuffless-calibration-free-blood-pressure-monitoring-technology-selected-to-present-at-american-college-of-cardiology-annual-scientific-session/]

Another technique was just disclosed by PyrAmes Inc. They detect the pressure of the pulse passing through the arteries. The pressure causes movement which is detected by a capacitive sensor**. Software needs to not only calculate the pressure but determine when the signal is not accurate. This was not a clinical study, so it still needs work before being used in a medical device.

[**in the journal Sensors, published by MDPI, Basel, Switzerland, June 2021]

Another technique, Pulse Transit Time, has been used, but has not achieved medical accuracy without calibration. It measures the time difference between the beat of the heart (measured with ECG electrodes) and the arrival of the pulse at an extremity (often measured with a PPG sensor). The time difference is proportional to the blood pressure. Although it is not medically accurate, it can be used in applications where the *change* in blood pressure is important, and the absolute value is not. Detecting a change is often important to indicate the need to take measures, such as visiting a healthcare provider.

Blood pressure has also been measured in a laboratory setting using the ECG signal and advanced neural network software. It is not medically accurate, however.

## Blood Glucose Measurement

The standard for blood glucose measurement is a sample of blood from the finger placed into a sensor. A very large amount of money has been expended to find a non-invasive glucose measurement technique. Today this has been partially achieved, although not fully, with continuous glucose monitors (CGM).

Abbott Diabetes has a small patch that is worn on the arm held in place with adhesive. It has a needle that passes through the skin to reach the blood, so it is technically invasive, but it is comfortable to wear for more than a week at a time. It requires calibration with a finger prick each time the disposable device is replaced. However, this is much more convenient than pricking your finger several times a day.

Another technique is a patch with microneedles. The microneedles only pass through the outer layer of the skin. They don't look or feel like needles. The texture is similar to sandpaper. It is challenging to get good results without intimate contact with the blood. This device also requires calibration.

Both sensors must be placed where there is good blood perfusion. They do not work on the wrist.

There are also implanted glucose monitors. However, most people prefer a less invasive device.

## Best Sensor Placements on the Body

Many wearable devices are designed to go on the wrist for convenience, but that is a poor place for most measurements.

ECG measurement is generally only done on the torso. The chest is clearly the best place because of proximity to the heart. Successful measurement in pants has been done using dry electrodes even when the person is moving. The Apple watch and other wrist-worn devices can only measure ECG when the opposite hand touches the watch, providing a signal that is from one arm to the other. This works well, but only while the watch is being touched.

PPG sensors for blood oxygen measurement requires good blood perfusion. The wrist is challenging, but it has been used successfully. Getting a pulse measurement from a PPG sensor is easier and can work nearly anywhere on the body.

Temperature measurement is best done under the arm, on the forehead, or in the ear. In general skin temperature is not reliably at the core body temperature, except at these locations. On the other hand, it can be useful to measure the temperature at extremities, not core body temperature, to detect problems with circulation and certain diseases.

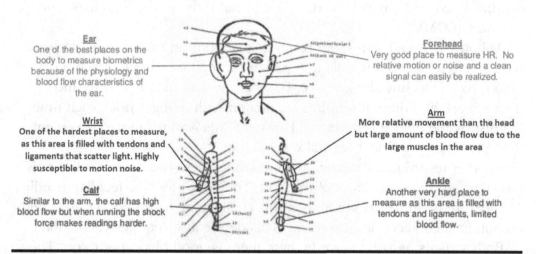

**Ear**
One of the best places on the body to measure biometrics because of the physiology and blood flow characteristics of the ear.

**Forehead**
Very good place to measure HR. No relative motion or noise and a clean signal can easily be realized.

**Wrist**
One of the hardest places to measure, as this area is filled with tendons and ligaments that scatter light. Highly susceptible to motion noise.

**Arm**
More relative movement than the head but large amount of blood flow due to the large muscles in the area

**Calf**
Similar to the arm, the calf has high blood flow but when running the shock force makes readings harder.

**Ankle**
Another very hard place to measure as this area is filled with tendons and ligaments, limited blood flow.

**Figure 11.1  PPG Sensor Placement.**

# Adhesives for Attachment

Since the torso is the best place for most measurements, there are many devices that attach to the torso. They usually use an adhesive patch. This is convenient, but there are limitations. A patch can only be applied to the skin for one or two weeks before the skin becomes irritated and begins to break down. For most applications, the adhesive needs to perform well while bathing or showering.

An alternative is to have sensors in a shirt. When the shirt is put on, the sensors begin recording and transmitting data. Shirts have limitations, too. They must be washed, and it is challenging to have electronics survive many times in a washing machine. Typically, devices are tested for 50 washes, but some clothing is washed more than that during its lifetime.

Sensors in a shirt need to be flexible, and ideally stretchable. Flexible circuits have been around for decades, but they need to be protected from moisture. Good sealing methods are more recent. Stretchable circuits are barely out of the laboratory. They are not yet widely used in wearable devices.

# Chapter 12

# Wireless Communication

Walter N. Maclay

Nearly all wearable devices communicate the sensor data through a wireless connection. There are some devices that use a connector to download data, but that means the data is not available immediately. Wireless communication can send the data in real time. There are many choices for wireless communication. The most used is Bluetooth Low Energy, or BLE. It uses the lowest power, and it can communicate directly to most smartphones. It must be within a few feet of the phone, however, so it will not work unless you take your phone wherever you go.

WiFi is convenient because it is available on all smartphones as well as hot spots in many places, but it consumes a lot of power, which requires a large battery. Cellular service can connect directly to the Internet rather than pass through a phone. This is a big advantage when a phone is not always being carried. Cellular uses a very large amount of power, however.

Battery life is a major limitation of wearable devices. To make the device small, the battery must be small; this means it does not last long between charges. A lot of design choices are made to minimize the power consumption. One of the biggest consumers of power is wireless communication.

One way to limit power is to send the data a very short distance to a smartphone. This is commonly done using Bluetooth Low Energy. It is the lowest power wireless communication for wearable devices, but it only works when the phone is nearby.

Another way to send data is through a gateway that connects to the Internet. WiFi uses hot spots or a phone as the gateway. There needs to be a gateway nearby, but the distance can be hundreds of feet, much more than

DOI: 10.4324/9781003304036-15

with BLE. WiFi is not generally a good match for wearable devices, however. It can transmit at very high speeds, but it uses a lot of power.

For many wearable devices the ideal wireless communication would send data directly to the Internet. Such wireless communication is available. There is a relatively new class of wireless called narrow band or Low Power Wide Area Network (LPWAN). This includes NB-IoT, LTE-M, LoRa, and Sigfox, among others. Narrow band communication transmits several kilometers at low power. The trade-off is a low data rate, but that is not a problem for most wearable devices. They rarely need to send more than a few hundred measurements per second, which is considered slow, and they often send less than one sample per second.

Table 12.1 compares various wireless standards. The data rate increases from left to right. The communication distance increases from top to bottom, and the power is shown as a number in milliwatts.

One important wireless standard is not shown in this table: NFC or Near Field Communication. It is similar to RFID, which is often used as a substitute for barcodes. NFC requires the transmitter to be within a few centimeters of the wearable device, and it requires no power from the wearable. The device doing the reading provides wireless power. Many smartphones

**Table 12.1   Power—How Much, How Far?**

|  | *100 bps* | *10K bps* | *40K bps* |
|---|---|---|---|
| 1 m | BLE4/Zigbee 0.15<br>BLE Mesh 0.15<br>Bluetooth 25<br>WiFi 50<br>LoRa 0.5 | BLE4/Zigbee 7.5<br>BLE Mesh 7.5<br>Bluetooth 25<br>WiFi 50<br>LoRa 10 | Zigbee 30<br>Bluetooth 25<br>WiFi 50<br>LoRa 20 |
| 50 m | Zigbee 20<br>WiFi 100<br>LoRa 0.5<br>Sigfox 0.5<br>NB-IoT, LTE-M 1.0<br>LTE, 5G Cellular 100 | Zigbee 30<br>WiFi 100<br>LoRa 20<br>NB-IoT, LTE-M 30<br>LTE, 5G Cellular 150 | WiFi 200<br>NB-IoT, LTE-M 200<br>LTE, 5G Cellular 200 |
| 1 km | LoRa 30<br>Sigfox 30<br>NB-IoT, LTE-M 20<br>LTE, 5G Cellular 120 | NB-IoT, LTE-M 100<br>LTE, 5G Cellular 200 | NB-IoT, LTE-M 400<br>LTE, 5G Cellular 400 |

*Source:* Voler Systems

**Table 12.2   Comparison of Wireless Communication Protocols.**

|  | LTE-M | NB-IOT | Sigfox | LoRa | BLE Mesh | Zigbee |
|---|---|---|---|---|---|---|
| Range | 1–50 km | 1–50 km | 10–50 km | 2–50 km | 10 m | 50 m |
| Data rate | 1 Mbit/s | 20–250 Kbit/s | 300 bit/s | 200–50 K bit/s | 20 Kbit/s | 40 Kbit/s |
| Supports Audio | Yes | Yes | No | No | No | Yes |
| Network | Public | Public | Public | Public or Private | Private | Private |
| Available | Good coverage | Good coverage | Limited coverage | Yes Limited public | Limited | Mature |

*Source:* Voler Systems

have NFC built in. They are often used to scan a device, such as a glucose monitor. The data is immediately visible on the phone from where it can be transmitted to the Internet to be shared.

Table 12.2 compares the most popular narrow band wireless communication with two other standards: Bluetooth LE Mesh, which is Bluetooth LE with the ability to communicate data through an array of devices to get greater range, and Zigbee, an older standard that transmits data similar distances to WiFi, but at much lower power. BLE Mesh and Zigbee are not narrow band wireless, and they are uncommon in wearable devices, but they are interesting to compare. LTE-M is also known as Cat-M1, LTE Cat-M1, or eMTC.

Notice that LTE-M can transmit as fast as 1Mbit/second, which is very fast for wearable devices. It is not advantageous at these speeds, as the power consumption approaches WiFi and cellular. Unlike WiFI and cellular, the power is much lower when the data rate is low. NB-IoT and LoRa are similar. They are very power-efficient when the data rate is very slow.

Another important differentiation with narrow band wireless is whether it uses a public or private network. A public network, such as the cellular network, has the advantage of easy roaming and no configuration of the network. The penalty is a monthly fee and the reliance on the network to exist. Sigfox has a major disadvantage here, as the network is very limited in the United States. LoRa has a big advantage in being able to run on a private network. This means you can install a network access point or hot spot in a school or factory, and you have LoRa service with no monthly charge. It doesn't matter that the LoRa public network is very limited in the United States.

Sigfox is primarily intended for one-way communication, from the wearable device to the Internet. It is popular in France and many European countries, but not in the United States or other countries. The limited public network makes it nearly unusable in most places. In recent years, NB-IoT and LTE-M have become widely available, making them an excellent choice for narrow band wireless.

NB-IoT has limitations when used in devices that move around, so LTE-M may be a better choice.

The coverage of LTE-M and NB-IoT around the world is shown here. When it is available in a country, that does not mean it is available everywhere. See Figure 12.1 for detailed coverage in the United States.

The coverage of NB-IoT in the United States is shown in Figure 12.2. In 2019, Verizon announced that they provided coverage for 92% of the population of the United States. It has grown since then. LTE-M has a similarly high coverage rate. At this high coverage rate, a manufacturer can successfully sell a product that uses it.

By comparison, Figure 12.3 shows the coverage for public networks for LoRa in the United States by Senet in early 2020. (Coverage data is difficult to get, so it was not possible to compare the coverage at the same points in time.)

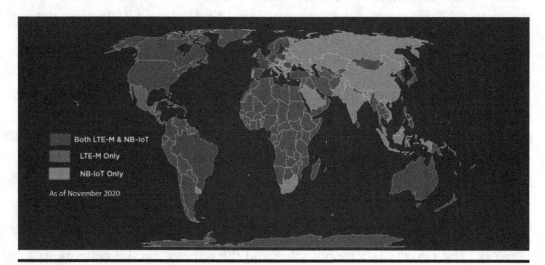

**Figure 12.1   NB-IoT and LTE-M Coverage Worldwide.**

*Source:* **GSM Association**

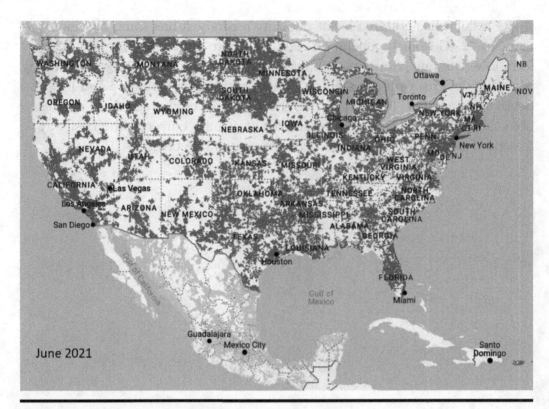

**Figure 12.2    NB-IoT and LTE-M Coverage in the USA.**

*Source:* Verizon

**Figure 12.3    LoRa Public Network Coverage in the USA.**

*Source:* Senet

5G cellular has gotten a lot of publicity recently. It has some big improvements over 4G (fourth generation cellular). There are claims that it will transform low data rate communication such as IoT (Internet of Things), including wearable devices. Unfortunately, 5G offers nothing for wearable and IoT devices at this time. The standard is still being developed for these applications. NB-IoT and LTE-M, which are part of 4G, are currently the best way to send data directly to the Internet from a wearable device.

## Chapter 13

# Batteries and Other Power Sources

Walter N. Maclay

## Contents

## Batteries

Nearly all wearable devices use batteries, and batteries are not improving very fast. If batteries had improved as fast as semiconductors over the last 50 years, you would be able to buy a battery the size of the head of a pin that would power your car and cost one cent!

This will never happen. Batteries are approaching the limit of chemical energy density. Figure 13.1 shows the relative capacity of several battery types compared to gasoline, which is nearly the highest energy density of any material. The horizontal scale is Megajoules per Liter. One Joule is the energy of one Watt for one second; barely enough to detect the temperature change at your fingertip. Notice that the chart is logarithmic, so the difference between the best battery and gasoline is more than 10 times. Gasoline, however, has serious safety issues. There is a trade-off between energy density and safety.

DOI: 10.4324/9781003304036-16

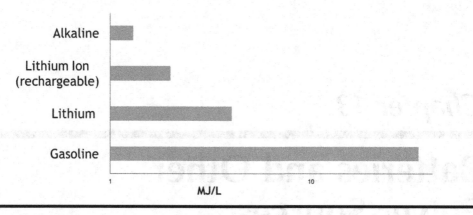

**Figure 13.1 Relative Capacity of Several Battery Types.**

*Source:* Voler Systems

   Lithium batteries are about as far as we are generally willing to go in sacrificing safety. There have been many news stories about lithium batteries catching fire. Lithium batteries require a safety circuit to protect them from catching fire or exploding. Even with the safety circuit, though, there have been cases where the batteries caught fire.

   The one technology that has a higher energy density than chemical is nuclear energy, but that is not going to be used in wearable devices in the foreseeable future!

   Since batteries are not improving, we must look at other ways to extend the time between recharging. There are five parts of a wearable device that can be major power consumers:

   Wireless communication
   Displays
   Sensors
   Microprocessors
   Software

The power usage of wireless communication is discussed in the chapter on Wireless Communication.

## Display Power

The power used by displays varies widely from grayscale LCD displays, like those on wrist watches, to color LED displays. See Figure 13.2.

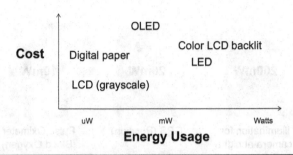

**Figure 13.2    Display Power vs Cost.**
*Source:* **Voler Systems**

Only grayscale LCD and digital paper are in the microwatt range, and they have limitations that often make them unsuitable. Digital paper is a rather new technology that consumes virtually no power unless the display is changing. It is ideal for mostly static displays like digital books. It is not able to display video. Digital paper also has only limited ability to display color.

Smartwatches usually use OLED technology, which is fairly energy-efficient, but it still can be a major power consumer in a wearable device. Like LEDs and color LCDs, OLED displays can have vivid colors and display video. The power consumption of these display technologies is a major reason displays are not used much in wearable devices.

## Sensor Power

The power used by sensors various widely as shown in Figure 13.3.

Cameras are power hogs, and even more so if they need illumination for use at night or inside dark places. They are widely used by police to record activity, but they cannot run continuously for an eight-hour shift without a really big battery. In addition, if the video is to be transmitted wirelessly, it requires a power-hungry technology such as WiFi or cellular.

GPS uses a moderate amount of power, as does a pulse oximeter. Pressure sensors can be quite low. Measuring ECG or EKG (electrocardiogram) is very low, as is a 9-axis motion sensor. Microphones and light intensity sensors can be even lower.

The lowest power is a 3-axis motion sensor. At just a few microwatts they are often left on, while other things are put in sleep mode to conserve

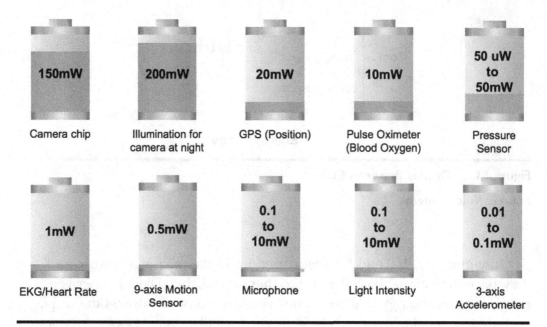

**Figure 13.3 Power Used by Sensors.**

*Source:* Voler Systems

power. The 3-axis motion sensor can activate the processor when a preset level of motion is detected. Then the processor can check the sensors, see what is going on, and decide if it needs to do anything. If not, it can quickly go back to sleep.

Because of their low power, low cost, and small size, motion sensors are put into all kinds of devices.

## Microprocessor Power

Microprocessor power consumption varies widely depending on the function of the processor. The processor in a Windows PC may consume 50 watts or more, but it can process real-time video. The processors used in wearable devices typically consume just a few milliwatts, and new models are being introduced that consume only microwatts of power. They are fine for most of the things that need to be done in a wearable device.

In order to limit power consumed by microprocessors, energy-intensive things like video processing and advanced encryption are usually not done in wearable devices.

# Software Power

Although software is not a physical device that consumes power, it runs in a processor and determines how much power the processor uses. Functions such as encrypting data can consume a lot of power while reading data from a sensor and storing it in memory consumes very little.

Software has another important role. It determines when devices are used. Sensors, for example, do not need to run all the time. Many physiological parameters, such as temperature and blood oxygen, change slowly. A measurement every minute or slower is usually sufficient. The rest of the time, the software can turn off the sensor. The software also directs the processor when to sleep and when to send data wirelessly. Thus, the software is critical to controlling the use of power.

Turning off the wireless communication has a trade-off called latency. If data is transmitted only once a minute, it takes a minute to get an update. This is a latency of one minute. If a person is waiting to see the data, one minute is a very long time. If a wearable device receives instructions wirelessly (for example, instructions to send data), the wireless receiver must not be sleeping, or it may miss the request. If it is sleeping, the request must be sent over and over until the device wakes up. If it wakes up once a minute, it also has a latency of one minute.

The solution to long latency is running the processor or wireless communication more, which consumes more power. When listening for a signal, the wireless communication only needs to be in receive mode, which consumes low power. Thus, the latency when waiting for a device to respond can be short without consuming a lot of power.

An alternative to batteries is to use energy harvesting. Power can be picked up from motion, temperature differences, chemical reactions, radio signals, and sunlight. The problem is that most sources of energy harvesting generate microwatts of power, while most wearable devices consume milliwatts of power. For this reason, most wearable devices do not use energy harvesting, although work is being done to improve energy harvesting.

Photocells for energy harvesting are well-known. They are used to power houses and calculators. You can get a lot of power, but there are some issues. To get milliwatts of power requires rather large cells. A photocell one square centimeter in size will generate about two milliwatts of power in direct sunlight perpendicular to the plane of the photocell. Also, wearable devices are used indoors or under clothes, where there is little light. For these reasons, they are rarely used on wearable devices.

Motion is a good source of energy. Wearable devices are often in motion. The motion can be converted to energy by crystals that output a voltage when under pressure. A small mass, such as a piece of steel placed next to the crystal, will alternately apply pressure or remove it when the device moves back and forth. One such device outputs up to 18 mW at 0.5 g of acceleration, which is an aggressive motion. At 0.1 g it only outputs 1 mW. It is 52 millimeters in diameter and 24 millimeters thick, and it costs about $50 in small quantities. The price is far more than the price of a battery, and the size is bigger than many batteries, making it unattractive in most applications.

Temperature differences generate energy when there are dissimilar metals exposed to the temperature difference. This is the Seebeck effect, which makes thermocouples work to measure temperature. For small temperature changes the output is quite small, so they are not used in wearable devices.

Radio signals contain power that can be picked up and converted to electrical energy. Wireless charging can transmit many watts of power over a few centimeters. It's difficult to transmit power very far, because the energy drops off as the square of the distance. This means that 10 watts at a distance of 1 cm would become 10 milliwatts at 10 meters. Wearable devices may not stay within 10 meters of a transmitter. Installing a wireless power transmitter is inconvenient, too. Power can be transmitted directionally at high frequencies, but the high frequencies are harmful to animals and people at useful power levels, thus this technology is not used much. It is possible to detect when an animal or person passes into the beam of the energy, but it must be ultra-reliable. Failure to turn off the beam could cause serious injury.

Chemical energy is sometimes used in implanted devices. The body is a great chemical factory and a source of power. The right materials can tap into the power. Although the power is quite limited, implanted devices are usually very low-power. For externally worn wearable devices, chemical energy is not used for energy harvesting.

# Chapter 14

# Cybersecurity

Walter N. Maclay

## Contents

Cybersecurity is a growing problem. Devices are being hacked more and more. When this happens, the data may be intercepted or corrupted. In addition, devices such as laptops, cell phones, and wearable devices can become portals into the networks of homes, businesses, and healthcare facilities.

94% of healthcare organizations have been the victim of a cyberattack*. As early as 2012, the TRENDnet webcam was hacked. The hackers posted livefeeds of 700 cameras to the Internet**. In 2017, St. Jude pacemakers were shown to be vulnerable to hacking. The hackers sold the stock short before they announced their hacking. As a result, 465,000 pacemakers were recalled. There was concern that hackers could deplete the battery early or even alter patients' heart rate***.

[*source: SANS Institute
**source: TechNewsWorld
***source: The Guardian]

Most consumer products have little cybersecurity. It costs money to make devices more secure, and consumers do not make purchasing decisions

DOI: 10.4324/9781003304036-17

based on the security of a device. This may change as security hacks grow in severity and frequency.

Wearable devices are more at risk of cyberattacks than devices that don't move. Not only can the data be intercepted, but a healthcare facility may not know that data is coming from a different device, or that the device may be worn by the wrong person. They also have all the issues that affect other devices. The data can be intercepted on the Internet if it's not encrypted. The device may be an easy way to get access to the internal network in order to attack it. The device may be spoofed by another device, so it can gain access to the data or internal network. A hacker may change settings on the device, so it behaves incorrectly. The data may not be accurate. The timestamp on the data may be incorrect.

Apple was quite careful about cybersecurity in its Apple Watch 4. It has capabilities that can make it a medical device, such as detecting falls or arrhythmia. To determine if the device is authorized to send data and that the right device is sending data, Apple:

1. Lets the user know they need to grant permission to send data.
2. Prompts the user with a health authorization dialog on their phone.
3. Sends data from the phone to authorize data transmission.
4. Tells the Apple Watch that the authorization was completed.

## FDA Cybersecurity

Medical devices do require protection from cyberattacks. The FDA issued a guidance document in 2014, which can be found at www.fda.gov/regulatory-information/search-fda-guidance-documents/content-premarket-submissions-management-cybersecurity-medical-devices-0. They also issued a draft update in 2018, although it still has not gone into effect as of late 2021: www.fda.gov/regulatory-information/search-fda-guidance-documents/content-premarket-submissions-management-cybersecurity-medical-devices. The 2018 document is more specific in its recommendations. It is not a totally new methodology. It's a good idea to use the 2018 document to be ready when it gets adopted.

Although guidance documents are not requirements, they should not be ignored. Following the guidance makes approval easier. Not following it may require justification.

The 2018 FDA guidance document has two tiers. Tier 1 is a higher level of security for

- Devices that connect to another product or network (wired or wirelessly)
- Where a cybersecurity incident could directly result in harm to multiple patients.

Tier 1 recommends the following.

- Authorization—ensure the user is authorized to use the device
- Authentication—verify the identity of the user
- Encryption—data is encrypted, and commands are encrypted
- Identification of security breaches
- Correction—fix the security breach and make the device resistant to similar breaches

More specifically, the Tier 1 recommendations include:

1. Prevent unauthorized use:
   a. Limit access to trusted users and devices only
   b. Authenticate and check authorization of safety-critical commands
2. Ensure trusted content by maintaining code, data, and execution integrity
3. Maintain confidentiality of data
4. Design the device to detect cybersecurity threats in a timely fashion
5. Design the device to respond to and contain the impact of a potential cybersecurity incident
6. Design the device to recover capabilities or services that were impaired due to a cybersecurity incident

In addition, Tier 1 design recommendations include:

- Cryptographic verification and authentication
- Secure configuration
- Cybersecurity BOM (CBOM)
- Patches and updates (rapid verification, validation testing, and deployment)

- Autonomous functionality
- Session timeout
- Intrusion detection system
- Routine security and antivirus scanning
- Forensic evidence capture
- Vulnerability analysis
- Breach notification
- Retention and recovery
- Other resilience measures

For details of the FDA requirements and recommendations, refer to the links listed to download the documents.

Tier 2 has the same recommendations, but items may be ignored if a risk-based rationale shows they are not appropriate.

## HIPAA—Patient Data Privacy

HIPAA requires patient data to be protected. It is separate from and different from cybersecurity, but you can't meet HIPAA without having good cybersecurity. Patient data security is very serious with strong punishments. HIPAA requires end-to-end security:

- From device to database
- Physical access control at the database

For wearable devices, the data needs less security if it is transmitted with only a patient code, not the identity of the patient. The patient's identity can be identified from the code when it is stored in the database.

## CE Cybersecurity

CE (the European Commission) has different cybersecurity requirements from the FDA. They are less specific than the FDA, but they are required, not just guidance. Devices must be safe, effective, and secure. There is a strong focus on data protection per GDPR, which is stricter than HIPAA in the US.

The documents that define the requirements include:

■ Annex I of the Medical Device Regulations (MDR)—safety and performance requirements: www.medical-device-regulation.eu/2019/07/23/annex-i-general-safety-and-performance-requirements/
■ EN62304—requirements for software
■ EN14971—requirements for hazard analysis

There are 8 "practices" required by CE:

■ Practice 1: security management
■ Practice 2: specification of security requirements
■ Practice 3: secure by design
■ Practice 4: secure implementation
■ Practice 5: security verification and validation testing
■ Practice 6: management of security-related issues
■ Practice 7: security update management
■ Practice 8: security guidelines—documentation

In addition, it is the manufacturer's responsibility to determine the minimum requirements for the operating environment regarding IT network characteristics and IT security measures that could not be implemented through the product design.*

[*from MDCG 2019–16 Guidance on Cybersecurity for medical devices, https://ec.europa.eu/health/sites/default/files/md_sector/docs/md_cybersecurity_en.pdf]

Elements to consider when adopting a security-by-design approach:

■ Lower cost
■ More resilient systems
■ Reduced risk of liability
■ Built-in rather than bolt-on security
■ Effective and early security flaws removal

This is the only way to meet FDA and CE cybersecurity requirements. As with other aspects of the design, you need to have clear requirements for cybersecurity. You need to evaluate risk, which may require changing the requirements. When the design is complete, you need to perform verification testing to show that the device meets the requirements.

Factors to consider when designing a wearable medical device:

- Try to use proven technology with less chance of security flaws
- Check for known exploits in the technology platform
- Perform risk assessment—break risk down into individual items each with the risk and effort required.
- Cryptography—what level of cryptography is needed? Too high requires more power and time
- Encryption—this is not just protecting data with an encryption algorithm. Key management is actually more important.
- Threat Detection—how can one detect a threat before any damage is done?
- Penetration Testing—hire ethical hackers who attempt to attack a system
- Developers—are they involved in threat modeling? Are they aware of your organization's secure-by-design practice?
- Maintainability—are requirements for maintainability and tools to measure it in place?
- Privacy by Design—is privacy included in your approach (HIPAA and GDPR)?
- Further Improvements—how can you continuously improve device development? Security will get more challenging during the life of the product.

# SUCCESSFUL APPLICATIONS

**4**

# Chapter 15

# Voice Technology and Wearables: Remote Patient Monitoring

Audrey Arbeeny

## Contents

The advent of many developments in the digital space and the focus on devices have laid out a landscape of opportunities in Voice Technology and Wearables. This segment is quickly growing and is very valuable to patients, healthcare providers, and caregivers.

Previously, patients may not have been able to stay in their own homes, or they had to endure tedious and frequent trips to their doctor's office. Now, many can be monitored from home, with the data transmitted directly to their healthcare provider. Families can be in contact to monitor the patient, and also gain access to the data through apps.

Some examples of popular wearable devices in healthcare include:

- Wearable fitness trackers that monitor many health conditions
- Smart health watches

DOI: 10.4324/9781003304036-19

- Wearable ECG monitors
- Wearable blood pressure monitors
- Wearable biosensors
- Sensor badges for healthcare providers
- Voice transcription devices for medical teams

This landscape is rapidly expanding, with more wearables, more sound and voice interaction, and the ability to enable consistent, long-term monitoring so the patient, senior, or end user's condition change can be detected immediately. Voice technology has played a major role in this, because not only can we monitor the need; we now have 1) a means of communication to ask what the readings are through our smart devices, and 2) a mechanism to interact, to learn what those readings mean, and to transmit the data to a healthcare provider.

Let's explore a few recent developments in health wearables and take a look at what the future may hold.

## Talking Blood Pressure Monitors

A new advancement is the talking blood pressure monitor. Major developers are expanding the capabilities that make it convenient for any patient or caregiver to use at home. These monitors also provide accessibility for the blind.

They not only give readings, but they also provide verbal alerts when pressure is not within range, and give full verbal instruction in several languages.

## Talking Glucose Monitoring Systems

Another area in full swing in devices is talking glucose monitoring systems, like the one pictured here. Voice is the premiere feature on this device.

This device is fully audible. There is a repeat button that replays the last message that was spoken in case the user missed something or wanted to be certain. It has tactile features for easy navigation, like raised and imprinted buttons, and it is accessible for those who are blind as well.

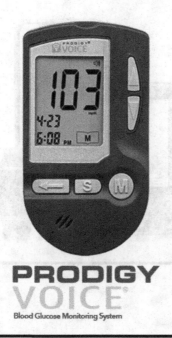

**Figure 15.1**

*Source:* www.prodigymeter.com/

## Dexcom G6 CGM System

This is a small wearable sensor and transmitter that sends glucose numbers to a smart device or receiver every 5 minutes. The user can see their glucose data in real time on compatible smart devices and share their data using Clarity, which is Dexcom's diabetes app. Data can be downloaded and sent to a physician. It has Siri integration, so the user can read the glucose numbers and display them in a graph.

Healthcare providers can also use this product to monitor the readings of their patients. A continuous glucose monitoring system (CGM) can be used for children 2 years of age and older.

## Voice Enabled Wearables for Practitioners

There are many technologies that significantly help the healthcare provider and make a deep impact on their efficiency and ability to communicate quickly. One example is the Vocera Smartbadge. This is a wearable badge

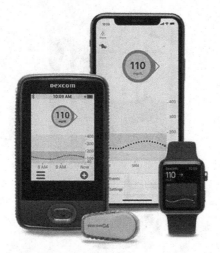

**Figure 15.2**

*Source:* **Dexcom.com**

**Figure 15.3**

*Source:* **Vocera.com**

for providers who need voice, text messaging, and alarm notifications with context about the patient, care team, and event. This makes it easy to reach someone for extra help, ask questions about a patient, or call for medication, amongst other things.

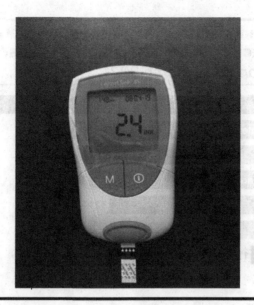

**Figure 15.4**

*Source* **photo Audrey Arbeeny**

## Medical Alert Systems

There are now monitoring systems that not only detect falls in a user wearing a pendant or wristband; they can also offer direct verbal communication through that device instead of a base that could be in another room or could be inaudible to the homebound person. Products like Medipendant® provide a speaker in the pendant, enabling the user to speak and listen directly through the pendant in the event of an emergency.

Roche Diagnostics' CoaguChek Meter is an easy-to-use system that checks blood clotting time. A drop of blood on a test strip yields results that are displayed on an LCD screen; results are called in, and the user receives a remote voice response. If the user doesn't submit results, they receive voice reminders and ultimately a phone call if no readings are submitted. This saves the patient from having to make a trip to their doctor to get this reading.

## Health Wearables Are Now Advancing into the Medical Space

Looking at the landscape of FitBit or Apple Watch and others, these devices were originally designed for style and some health benefits. Now these

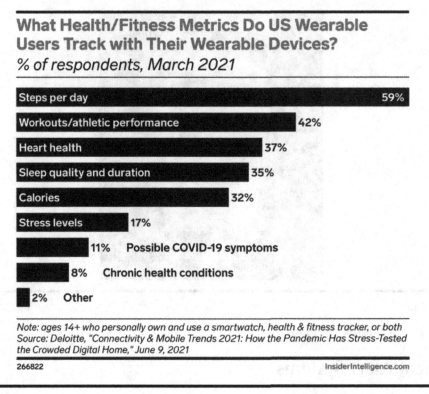

**What Health/Fitness Metrics Do US Wearable Users Track with Their Wearable Devices?**
% of respondents, March 2021

| | |
|---|---|
| Steps per day | 59% |
| Workouts/athletic performance | 42% |
| Heart health | 37% |
| Sleep quality and duration | 35% |
| Calories | 32% |
| Stress levels | 17% |
| Possible COVID-19 symptoms | 11% |
| Chronic health conditions | 8% |
| Other | 2% |

Note: ages 14+ who personally own and use a smartwatch, health & fitness tracker, or both
Source: Deloitte, "Connectivity & Mobile Trends 2021: How the Pandemic Has Stress-Tested the Crowded Digital Home," June 9, 2021

266822                                                    InsiderIntelligence.com

**Figure 15.5**

devices, along with health tracking devices like Amazon Halo and other wearables, have become an imperative central hub for gathering critical medical information and transmitting it to a smartphone, caregiver, or healthcare provider.

This holds true for Alexa and Google as well, where caretakers and healthcare providers can access data. Nearly all the big tech companies have integrated new technologies that enable a user to connect to their smart device and ask questions about their readings. And they are investing heavily in the medical field and integrated devices.

## Apple Watch System 7

Apple debuted this larger-faced watch, which will be available in October 2021.

As with the 2020 model, there is a blood-oxygen sensor, a built-in ECG app, heart rate notifications, and fall detection. It will provide alert notifications if there is an irregularity.

**Figure 15.6**

*Source:* https://support.apple.com/guide/watch/track-important-health-information-apple-apd0d5d452ce/watchos

The FitBit Sense Smartwatch with Voice Assistant comes already integrated with Google Assistant and Amazon Alexa so users can ask questions about their results.

## Smart Health Trackers

Health trackers are also on the rise, and they integrate with a user's voice through their smartphone or other smart devices. For example, Amazon debuted a new feature in March 2021 for its Halo health-tracking device: integration with Amazon Alexa that lets users call up information on their health data via voice command.

Halo uses advanced sensors that collect health data, including temperature, heart rate, sleep, and fitness activity. The Halo device has two microphones that can also be turned on or off at the user's discretion to analyze energy and positivity in the speaker's voice. By integrating with Amazon Alexa, Halo owners can link their wearable with the voice assistant and will be able to give vocal commands asking Alexa devices about their health metrics collected by Halo.

The Oura Ring uses very advanced sensor technology and a mobile app to deliver a host of health measurements and insights. It is one of the only products that measures a user's temperature directly from their skin. It measures resting heart rate and heart rate variability, respiratory rate, light, deep and REM sleep, nighttime movement, sleep timing, and sleep quality.

Its Cura app is free for both iOS and Android users. It is compatible with Google Fit as well as Apple's Health App, with many robust measurements that can be shared (encrypted) with family or healthcare providers.

The Apple Health App integrates a host of data with technology that healthcare providers are already using. And it goes beyond the usual measurements and readings that most other devices measure, as it is a great communication tool for sharing vital health information.

## Conclusion

So what does all this indicate? We now have the ability for many to age in place, get services remotely, and communicate directly with caregivers, family, and healthcare professionals from home. The National Institute on Aging is a valuable source of information for consumers to learn about and integrate these devices, so their loved ones can stay in their homes. And while some adults may prefer the level of help available in senior communities, the vast majority of the aging population wants to remain in their homes for as long as possible. According to an AARP study, 90 percent of people aged 65 and over want to remain in their own homes as they get older, and not go to a nursing home or assisted living facility.

And the same holds true for younger patients who are homebound, have special health conditions, or are dependent on medical care and monitoring. Technological advances will help make that desire a reality for many, regardless of their age.

All of this indicates a continued convergence of a variety of technologies to advance remote patient monitoring. Voice Technology and Wearables will bring us great advances in healthcare. This was my prediction in 2020, and it is even stronger now.

My prediction is that we'll see the most growth going to the healthcare industry: developments such as synthetic voices, the ability to interpret emotional nuances, predictive behavior, medical robotics, devices, home monitoring, and patient/caregiver interaction. All these seem to be emerging the fastest. This is because of the rapid growth from smart speaker to machine learning and adaption of the technology, UI, UX, and the new capabilities that are evolving every day. We now have a large aging population with caregivers and healthcare providers who need more remote monitoring, wellness check-ins, and interactions. The list goes on.

Related reading: Connecting Beyond Voice Through Sonic Branding

# Chapter 16

# Connected Device for Improved Adherence

Chris Landon MD, FAAP, FCCP, FRSM

## Contents

In our pre-work to developing such devices as the Bodimetrics Circul
Ring, we began with Bluetooth Health, rather than the wellness devices, to
understand what we needed to measure and whether that would result in
changes. Utilized in the Hill-Rom airway clearance device and in the medication nebulization device, we saw the benefits of being able to look into a
patient's bedroom.

A monitoring feature was incorporated into an electronic nebulizer to
provide physicians and caregivers with a tool to reliably assess and optimize
patient adherence to treatment using motivational interviewing. The eTrack
controller (PARI Pharma, Germany) was used with Altera and eFlow rapid
handsets to nebulize Cayston (Gilead) and other cystic fibrosis (CF) drugs
per individual. Data of nebulizations were transferred automatically and
remotely to the RedCap database, an adherence dashboard for physician and
patient. The device was used for 20 subjects aged 8–32 with low adherence.
Rapid feedback was provided (1) as part of a depression intervention with
reward for adherence, (2) for bringing adherence in line prior to initiation
of Orkambi, (3) after the patient had regressed, and (4) for dispensing the
medication delivery into another language and culture. Clinical data: Lung
function test (spirometry, %FEV1, Pulmonary Exacerbation Score), and Body

Mass Index (BMI) improved from baseline in all subjects. For both % FEV1 and PES, 21.4% of subjects improved significantly, as assessed by the Reliable Change Index. Conclusion: The device allows co-care—active engagement by the patient and provider of the treatment and shared decision-making in individualizing therapy for each patient's schedule, creating a pathway toward cognitive behavioral therapy intervention. Weekly review of adherence is studied as a process, as opposed to the quarterly team review, by patient recall and medication possession by refill data. This additional communication between patient and CF team addresses the challenges of adhering to treatments collaboratively, thus avoiding misunderstandings about the therapy. The device has potential to replace pharmacy refill histories and Daily Phone Diaries. The pilot study demonstrates that Electronic Monitors can become the "gold standard" and can be integrated into current delivery systems.

## Ecosystem

Whether for Consumer (Wellness) or Professional (Health), there is now a dependence on the smartphone as the entry point for data from the wearable, with the future integration directly into the HER. Both approaches, for wellness or health, rely on the assumption of data security. The secure data server needs to provide an End User Portal, an Application Programming Interface (API) for research with revocable access, and a secure API to defend against personal health information attacks. Within that Secure Data Server lies an additional layer of Machine Learning, Natural Language Processing, and algorithms for sleep, exercise, nutrition, activity, stress, and other captured variables from the wearables that can be used for health and wellness application and intervention. In a population-based health and wellness information interpretation, the data must be aggregated, and ambiguity and duplication addressed to provide an interpretable data set. Between and within institutions there must be governance with set policies for enforcement and consent management. This allows individual and aggregate medical socio-economic systems and data to emerge.

# Chapter 17

# COVID-19 Wellness Monitoring Turns to Health Monitoring

Chris Landon MD, FAAP, FCCP, FRSM

I became involved in the evolution of personal vital sign monitoring in the 1990s with Vivometrics. Using a gorgeous vest with Lifeshirt written vertically across the zipper, we integrated heart rate, respiratory rate with respiratory inductive plethysmography, blood pressure, pulse oximetry, and other measures DARPA won't let me talk about. With algorithms derived from my asthma, COPD, and cystic fibrosis patients, we home monitored and interpreted sleep in first responders, race car drivers, astronauts, and athletes. At fifteen thousand dollars per Lifeshirt, our business model depended on big Pharma research, grants, and CMS recognizing home sleep studies at a rate that matched the costs. Unfortunately, the 2008 economic meltdown led to the decrease in funding from these sources. CMS didn't recognize home sleep studies until it met their economic model. The software was recreated and is used in the study of early intervention for neuromuscular diseases, and the cost of the form factor has dropped to ten percent of what it was.

Extraordinary developments allowed the long-anticipated break-out moment for remote patient monitoring. CMS has provided billing codes for Medicare that allow the dispensing of devices, human counseling based on the device's readings, and a long-term proposition of clinic investment in devices which pay for themselves with continued use.

DOI: 10.4324/9781003304036-21

In dealing constantly with wearable startups, I have, unfortunately, seen many unique ideas that have received sweat equity, friends, fools and family financing, and very clever and triumphant code writers with vast knowledge of Apple software been brought to their knees by the constant changing of the Apple iOS or Android not being available or not working among the family of devices.

That all started to change last year when the Centers for Medicare and Medicare Services (CMS) changed its reimbursement rules to make Remote Patient Monitoring (RPM) more accessible. Then COVID-19 came along and made it essential. There will be a retreat from telehealth payment by insurers as the pandemic slows down.

Sheltering in place has turned over the rock of the need for more frequent and convenient visits to monitor lab and remote patient monitoring tools for seniors and patients with chronic diseases. Due to this shift, this population has simply not been exposed to influenza, RSV, rhinovirus, and other transmissible respiratory diseases. Remote patient monitoring allows even patients who are non-critical COVID-19-positive to continue to be monitored at home. Even in my clinic, I am only getting a two-minute snapshot. Augmenting the telehealth visit with digital scale, oximetry, blood pressure, heart rate, respiratory rate, sleep study, and exercise capability allows a ten-thousand-foot view. Plus, with the addition of machine learning, there is the added ability to predict exacerbations.

Beyond reducing admissions and allowing earlier discharge, the true goal is preventing readmissions. Improving patient outcomes requires improved compliance rates and patients taking ownership of their own healthcare. This provides a different target than wellness, moving it to health with measurable consequences of remote patient monitoring. The Chronic Care Management Program of CMS has been predicated on these assumptions and, in targeted high utilizations, has shown benefit. See https://mathematica. org/publications/evaluation-of-the-diffusion-and-impact-of-the-chronic-care-management-ccm-services-final-report.

COVID-19 has only underlined the direction CMS has taken from reimbursing remote monitoring in rural or remote areas to the 2018 99091 reimbursement code. We have participated in the predecessor program through the United States Department of Agriculture Rural Utilities Service Distance Learning and Telemedicine Program, aimed at keeping farmers in their hometowns. The cost of equipment and expansion of bandwidth were supported, but with a cohort of physician champions that left after two years of service, it has been a difficult journey. The unfounded comprehensive grant writing and project administration process, the project funds being advanced by the applying organization, and the lack of support for actual physician consultation services has made it a difficult program for us to continue to be a part of. The new CMS reimbursement rules, extended to include chronic disease or coronavirus, have been extended by some private insurers as well.

Beyond usable, actionable data, the key has been improved ease of use. Heart rate, movement, and sleep patterns are built into wearables through form factors such as the watch; Bluetooth-connected blood pressure cuffs, blood glucose monitors, and weight scales upload through smartphones and tablets. Two hurdles have been identified in asking what to do with all this information. Information overload for the physicians was clearly demonstrated to me when I was approached, politely, by Canadian physicians at a conference. They asked me what I wanted them to do with three hundred blood pressure records every Monday that they needed to review if they accepted them and were responsible for any missed pathology. This led to better guidelines, clinically intuitive screens based on patient goals of reduced systolic hypertension, and new medication changes, which in the face of "white coat hypertension" might lead to hypotension at home.

The failure of electronic healthcare records to accept the data directly, leading to scanned-in PDF documents, is now being more directly addressed by the CURES Act.

The mandate, a rare piece of bipartisan legislation, was signed into law in 2016 to: increase choice and access for patients and providers, to streamline development and delivery for drugs and medical devices, to accelerate research into serious illnesses, to address the opioid crisis, and to improve mental health services. A balance between decreasing regulatory burdens associated with the EHR and health information technology and advancing interoperability concentrated on a key sales strategy used by the EHR vendors—lack of interoperability. Information blocking by preventing and interfering with access to health information, exchange of health information, and input of information from devices forced institutions to choose an EHR with a silo. By April 15, 2021, it finally took effect, having passed through the ONC, CMS, and HHS. When a patient asks for their data elements, there are mandated options available:

- Printing the data from the EHR
- Exporting it through a Continuity of Care Document (CCD) in the EHR
- Directing patients to view and download data using a patient portal

With the data elements seen here: www.healthit.gov/isa/united-states-core-data-interoperability-uscdi#uscdi-v1

The so-called ONC Final Rule, beyond data sharing, puts pressure on remote health monitoring wearables to support Application Program Interface (API) functionality and to certify the health IT through the ONC Health IT Certification Program in order to bring about standardization. The development of this API token/electronic key makes it possible for software applications to connect. This alone did not solve the problem, as there isn't a consistent way to plug an API token into an app such as Apple Health. The goal of the Cures Act, to allow a new market of health apps to leverage data from any electronic healthcare record in a single standard non-proprietary format, is underway through Fast Healthcare Interoperability Resources (FHIR).

This makes it easier than ever for patients to gather and share health data—and for physicians to make sense of it. Unlike the diabetic logbooks of old, physicians don't need to scan rows of handwritten numbers looking for patterns. Nor do they need to scan spreadsheets of data from patients' smartwatches and fitness trackers. Instead, the data is run through algorithms that spot patterns, note trends, and even apply predictive analytics to warn about future problems. Physicians get this information in real time, not when the patient comes back for a checkup—or worse, when the patient gets readmitted to the hospital.

Some RPM providers are also integrating their solutions with electronic health records (EHR) systems. That way, physicians can view data and insights from the remote monitoring data solution inside the EHR, along with the patient's other pertinent health information. And with the right clinical communications solution in place, physicians can even receive mobile alerts if a patient's data needs immediate attention.

But it's not just patient data. It's actionable data—the kind that improves patient care and their healthcare experience.

As a consultant to startups for over three decades, the recurring theme is "no money no mission." The investment to develop the API, the fees for FHIR access in each EHR, providing app updates with every twist of the Apple IOS or Android update, algorithms to provide actionable information, personal health information security, and the Cures Act mandates for large healthcare organizations, makes justifying the investment through demonstrable improvements in patient care essential.

Hand in hand is patient acceptance. The failure of the Prometheus adherence Bluetooth pill wasn't so much technology-based, but based in targeting a medication for schizophrenia and expecting wary patients with a borderline grasp of reality and technology to accept it. This is not that different from targeting potentially complicated technology use for other chronically ill elderly patients. If I were to look in my patients' windows to see how they are doing, they would call the police and I would be in an ankle bracelet.

But now, wearable photoplethysmography has evolved into an easy-to-use, patient-acceptable remote patient monitoring device. As the industry continues to evolve, the routine use of wearables becomes possible as cost comes down and continuous use throughout a daily, weekly, monthly, and yearly regimen is met with new form factors and battery technology. Previously formally relegated to expensive attended sleep labs, a solution for people with sleep problems, individuals with diagnosed sleep disorders in need of compliance and device effectiveness, occupational health screening and job-site monitoring, chronic lung disease, heart disease, and pre- and post-OVID-19 patients all will introduce us to routine monitoring. (Reference 1 Telemonitoring in continuous positive airway pressure-treated patients improves delay to first intervention and early compliance: a randomized trial. F. Hoet et al Sleep Med 2017;39:77–83)

There is a significant technical problem, however, with the smart bracelet and smartwatch, which are dependent on reflectance pulse oximetry. Restricted to the radial artery, there is a lot of real estate that needs to be cinched down, like avoiding ambient light and working around signal-to-noise ratio difficulties. Utilizing the palmar digital artery in the form of a ring allows accurate, continuous, and usable data independent of pigmentation. Black patients, utilizing the finger pulse oximeter, had nearly three times the occult hypoxemia as White patients (NEJM article Sjoding et al). This was sufficient enough to lead to an FDA Safety Communication in February 2021 as these values became even more critical in patient triage in the face of the COVID-19 epidemic. (Figure 17.1

Without a nasal thermistor, the clinicians' familiarity with the Apnea Hypopnea Index is shifted to the Oxygen Desaturation Index. The subjective symptoms of sleep apnea are reflected in hypoxemia but do not provide information about apnea length and depth. This leads to a closer correlation to the Epworth Sleepiness Scale, reflecting the clinical implications. This allows for screening prior to referral to a sleep center capable of close observation and intervention.

Overnight pulse oximetry in cardiorespiratory patients, inpatient and outpatient, provides an affordable solution with large clinical implications in monitoring the effect of CPAP or surgical intervention for OSAS. Additionally, nocturnal hypoxemia suggests poor prognosis in neuromuscular disease,

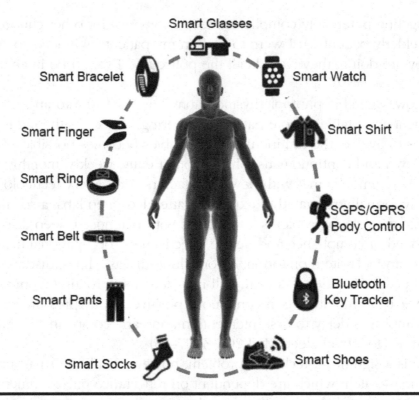

**Figure 17.1 But What Wearables? "Smart" is the Catchword for Glasses, Watch, Shirt, Shoes, Socks, Pants, Belt, Finger, Ring, Bracelet, GPS Backpack, and Bluetooth Key Tracker.**

*Source:* **www.gkmit.co/blog/mobile-development/wearable-technology-and-it-s-past-present-and-future**

COPD, and interstitial lung disease and provides early warning signal for supportive intervention with non-invasive ventilation. (Figure 17.2)

In the face of COVID-19, my multi-disciplinary Cystic Fibrosis clinic is often virtual, with a digital scale, Mir Bluetooth spirometer, pulse oximetry, exercise wearables, and handheld camera to look in refrigerators, observe exercise, conduct psychological counseling, and so forth. The problem now is finding the right platform to match smartphone type and bandwidth for patients and providers in their own homes. When we did patient surveys on acceptance of telehealth visits, unexpectedly, we found the overwhelming majority of adult patients would like to continue with these beyond COVID-19. This was in contrast to our pediatric patients' parents who wanted at least biannual in-person visits.

What I believe will lead to the development of the ecological system, aided by over half the over-65 demographic now owning smartphones,

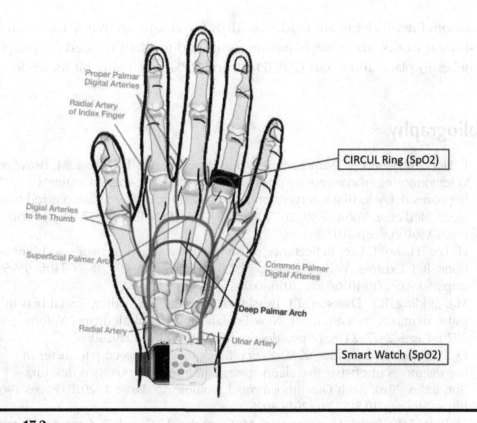

**Figure 17.2**
*Source:* **Porta-Medical**

is the investment by Pharma. We have found that COVID-19, without in-office visits, has made patient recruitment much more difficult by tele-phone, although our elderly patients do like to talk. Organizations as diverse as Science 37 and IQVia need to be able to: provide remote access to patients (now recruited through Facebook groups and other digital platforms), on-board doctors and patients via teleconferencing, obtain data through remote patient monitoring, and provide these devices and information-gathering to a non-tech-savvy population. Now, however, this process is happening in an accelerated setting of patient acceptance due to COVID-19.

Coronavirus fears have also made patients more interested in telehealth solutions such as RPM and virtual visits. Fifty-nine percent of consumers say they are more likely to use telehealth services now than before COVID-19, according to a recent Black Book Market Research survey.

Bottom line: Patients are ready for RPM, physicians are ready for it, studies show it works, and CMS is paying for it. Add to that the need for people to shelter in place and avoid COVID-19, and RPM has finally hit its stride.

# Bibliography

1. F. Hoet, W. Libert, C. Sanida, S. Van den Broecke, A.V. Bruyneel, M. Bruyneel, Telemonitoring in continuous positive airway pressure-treated patients improves delay to first intervention and early compliance: a randomized trial, Sleep Medicine, Volume 39, 2017, Pages 77–83, ISSN 1389–9457, https://doi.org/10.1016/j.sleep.2017.08.016.
2. H. Lee, H. Ko, J. Lee, Reflectance pulse oximetry: practical issues and limitations, ICT Express, Volume 2, Issue 4, 2016, Pages 195–198, ISSN 2405–9595, https://doi.org/10.1016/j.icte.2016.10.004.
3. M.J. Sjoding, R.P. Dickson, T.J. Iwashyna, S.E. Gay, T.S. Valley, Racial bias in pulse oximetry measurement, New England Journal of Medicine, Volume 383, 2020, Pages 2477–2478, https://doi.org/10.1056/NEJMc2029240.
4. D. Temirbekov, S. Güneş, Z.M. Yazıcı, I. Sayın, The ignored parameter in the diagnosis of obstructive sleep apnea syndrome: the oxygen desaturation index, Turk Arch Otorhinolaryngol, Volume 56, Issue 1, 2018, Pages 1–6, https://doi.org/10.5152/tao.2018.3025.
5. N. Rashid, S. Zaghi, M. Scapuccin, M. Camacho, V. Certal, R. Capasso, The value of oxygen desaturation index for diagnosing obstructive sleep apnea: a systematic review, The Laryngoscope, Volume 131, Issue 2, 2020, https://doi.org/10.1002/lary.28663.
6. R. Downey 3rd, R.M. Perkin, J. MacQuarrie, Upper airway resistance syndrome: sick, symptomatic but underrecognized, Sleep, Volume 16, Issue 7, 1993, Pages 620–623, https://doi.org/10.1093/sleep/16.7.620. PMID: 8290854.
7. B. Jurado-Gamez, J.L. Gomez-Chaparro, M. Muñoz-Calero, A.S. Sanz, I. Muñoz-Cabrera, J. Lopez-Barea, D. Gozal, Serum proteomic changes in adults with obstructive sleep apnoea, Journal of Sleep Research, Volume 21, Issue 2, 2012, Pages 139–146, https://doi.org/10.1111/j.1365-2869.2011.00955.x.

# Conclusion

Michael W. Davis

The COVID-19 pandemic has clearly framed the need, viability, and effectiveness of remote patient monitoring (RPM) to advance healthcare delivery and services globally. RPM solutions enabled both providers and patients to safely interact in a timely manner to manage healthcare issues. Coupled with telemedicine/telehealth solutions, RPM provided a healthcare delivery capability that approached that of an in-person visit with a physician.

Current and future uses of RPM will continue to grow unabated for years to come. Advances of smartwatches, smartphones, and smart homes will allow healthcare delivery to be highly tailored to the patient's needs and lifestyle. RPM solutions will create a significant link for delivering a continuum of care healthcare environment that will improve healthcare access, reduce costs, and improve care quality and safety. An added benefit of RPM will be the addition of patient clinical data that can be analyzed to drive new and improved care delivery and evidence-based medicine protocols.

A key catalyst for RPM use and acceptance by consumers and clinicians is the advancement of standards and regulations that remove adoption concerns by both parties. These standards and regulations must be technology-agnostic to ensure the continued innovations of RPM solutions. Effective standards and regulations will enforce patient safety and should minimize regulatory certification processes that impact time-to-market efforts by vendors.

Regulatory efforts related to clinician reimbursement for using and managing RPM solutions are also a significant factor in driving RPM adoption

DOI: 10.4324/9781003304036-22

and use. CMS is aware of this need and is proposing new billing codes to facilitate higher levels of use of RPM for Medicare patients. These reimbursement activities will influence private insurers to also adopt improved reimbursements for RPM use by their members. Increased reimbursement models will ultimately drive higher RPM use that will drive higher levels of remote care delivery and improved patient outcomes that reduce population healthcare costs. Consumer demand for these services will also provide an economy of scale for providers to deliver these services with a profitability factor.

Technology advancements will continue to positively impact the components of RPM devices to drive down their costs, improve their reliability, and deliver devices that are easily adopted by consumers. RPM devices will become smaller to accommodate consumer needs and able to capture multiple clinical measures supporting better care management by clinicians. 5G cellular communications will expand the capabilities of RMP devices to exchange data with care providers, especially in areas where WiFi capabilities are limited or in rural environments. Battery technology will deliver more powerful and smaller batteries that can deliver their power more efficiently and charge up more quickly. Cybersecurity technology will continue to be a challenge for healthcare IT environments. Advances in IoMT security and provider enterprise security are reducing security threats but are not bulletproof. Cybersecurity will continue to be an environment that will require significant analysis for implementing interoperability services with RPM solutions to mitigate security threat risks.

Successful applications of RPM solutions and services are expanding dramatically. Many studies can be found relating the integration of RPM solutions with provider EHR environments to better monitor and manage chronic health risks. The use of RPM for monitoring C-19 infections related to patient temperatures and O2 saturation was adopted by many providers to determine if patients should be admitted or if they could be managed in their homes. Ongoing provider RPM research will continue to identify successes and failures with RPM that can be used to improve RPM devices and services. Key factors for RPM success for providers will be the ability to effectively integrate the data from RPM devices into the EHR in real-time, use artificial intelligence for clinical decision support to reduce clinician review overhead, and create clinician workflows that allow for ease of use and adoption of RPM data in the care delivery process. The effective interoperability of RPM with telemedicine/telehealth solutions and the EHR will provide a continuum of care environment that supports the CMS quadruple aim:

- Enhance patient experience,
- improve population health,
- reduce costs,
- and improve the work life of healthcare providers, including clinicians and staff.

# Glossary of Terms

**3G:** the third generation of wireless mobile telecommunications technology. It is the upgrade for 2.5G GPRS and 2.75G EDGE networks, for faster data transfer. This is based on a set of standards used for mobile devices and mobile telecommunications use services and networks that comply with the International Mobile Telecommunications-2000 (IMT-2000) specifications by the International Telecommunication Union. 3G finds application in wireless voice telephony, mobile Internet access, fixed wireless Internet access, video calls, and mobile TV.

**4G:** the fourth generation of broadband cellular network technology, succeeding 3G, and preceding 5G. A 4G system must provide capabilities defined by ITU in IMT Advanced. Potential and current applications include amended mobile web access, IP telephony, gaming services, high-definition mobile TV, video conferencing, and 3D television.

**5G:** the fifth-generation technology standard for broadband cellular networks, which cellular phone companies began deploying worldwide in 2019, and is the planned successor to the 4G networks which provide connectivity to most current cellphones. 5G networks are predicted to have more than 1.7 billion subscribers worldwide by 2025, according to the GSM Association. Like its predecessors, 5G networks are cellular networks, in which the service area is divided into small geographical areas called cells. All 5G wireless devices in a cell are connected to the Internet and telephone network by radio waves through a local antenna in the cell. The main advantage of the new networks is that they will have greater bandwidth, giving higher download speeds, eventually up to 10 gigabits per second (Gbit/s).

**802.11 a,b,c:** is part of the IEEE 802 set of local area network (LAN) technical standards, and specifies the set of media access control (MAC) and physical layer (PHY) protocols for implementing wireless local area network (WLAN) computer communication. The standard and amendments provide the basis for wireless network products using the Wi-Fi brand and are the world's most widely used wireless computer networking standards. IEEE 802.11 is used in most home and office networks to allow laptops, printers, smartphones, and other devices to communicate with each other and access the Internet without connecting wires. The a, b, c, and other letters define extensions to the standard.

**802.15.4 standard:** a technical standard that defines the operation of low-rate wireless personal area networks (LR-WPANs). It specifies the physical layer and media access control for LR-WPANs, and is maintained by the IEEE 802.15 working group, which defined the standard in 2003. It is the basis for the Zigbee, ISA100.11a, WirelessHART, MiWi, 6LoWPAN, Thread and SNAP specifications, each of which further extends the standard by developing the upper layers which are not defined in IEEE 802.15.

**Access point:** a networking hardware device that allows other wireless devices to connect to a wired network.

**Application Programming Interface (API):** is a connection between computers or between computer programs. It is a type of software interface, offering a service to other pieces of software. A document or standard that describes how to build or use such a connection or interface is called an API specification. A computer system that meets this standard is said to implement or expose an API. The term API may refer either to the specification or to the implementation.

**Barcodes:** a method of representing data in a visual, machine-readable form. Initially, barcodes represented data by varying the widths and spacings of parallel lines. These barcodes, now commonly referred to as linear or one-dimensional (1D), can be scanned by special optical scanners, called barcode readers, of which there are several types. Later, two-dimensional (2D) variants were developed, using rectangles, dots, hexagons, and other patterns, called matrix codes or 2D barcodes, although they do not use bars as such.

**Blood pressure cuff:** A sphygmomanometer (/ˌsfɪɡmoʊməˈnɒmɪtə/ SFIG-moh-mə-NO-mi-tər), also known as a blood pressure monitor, or blood pressure gauge, is a device used to measure blood pressure, composed of an inflatable cuff to collapse and then release the artery under the cuff in a controlled manner,[1] and a mercury or aneroid manometer to measure the pressure.

**Bluetooth Low Energy (BLE):** a wireless personal area network technology designed and marketed by the Bluetooth Special Interest Group (Bluetooth SIG) aimed at novel applications in the healthcare, fitness, beacons, security, and home entertainment industries. Compared to Classic Bluetooth, Bluetooth Low Energy is intended to provide considerably reduced power consumption and cost while maintaining a similar communication range. Mobile operating systems including iOS, Android, Windows Phone, and BlackBerry, as well as macOS, Linux, Windows 8, and Windows 10, natively support Bluetooth Low Energy.

**Clinical Document Architecture (CDA):** is a popular, flexible markup standard developed by Health Level 7 International (HL7) that defines the structure of certain medical records, such as discharge summaries and progress notes, as a way to better exchange this information between providers and patients. These documents can include text, images, and other types of multimedia—all integral parts of electronic health records (EHRs).

**Chronic Care Management (CCM):** encompasses the oversight and education activities conducted by healthcare professionals to help patients with chronic diseases and health conditions such as diabetes, high blood pressure, systemic lupus erythematosus, multiple sclerosis, and sleep apnea learn to understand their condition and live successfully with it. This term is equivalent to disease management for chronic conditions.

**Clinical Decision Support (CDS):** is a health information technology, that provides clinicians, staff, patients, or other individuals with knowledge and person-specific information, intelligently filtered or presented at appropriate times, to enhance health and healthcare. CDS encompasses a variety of tools to enhance decision-making in the clinical workflow. These tools include computerized alerts and reminders to care providers and patients; clinical guidelines; condition-specific order sets; focused patient data reports and summaries; documentation templates; diagnostic support, and contextually relevant reference information, among other tools.

**CMS Interoperability and Patient Access Rules:** As of July 1, 2021, two of the policies from the May 2020 Interoperability and Patient Access final rule are now in effect. On April 30, 2021, the requirements for hospitals with certain EHR capabilities to send admission, discharge and transfer notifications to other providers went into effect. On July

1, 2021, CMS began to enforce requirements for certain payers to support Patient Access and Provider Directory APIs.

**Connected Home Over IP (CHIP):** A Smart Home standard by Amazon, Apple, Google, and the Zigbee Alliance to simplify development for manufacturers and increase compatibility for consumers.

**Continuous Glucose Monitors (CGM):** Continuous glucose monitoring automatically tracks blood glucose levels, also called blood sugar, throughout the day and night. Patients can see their glucose level anytime at a glance. Patients can also review how their glucose changes over a few hours or days to see trends.

**Computer Memory:** a device or system that is used to store information for immediate memory; is often synonymous with the term primary storage or main memory. Computer memory operates at a high speed compared to disk storage, which is slower but offers higher capacities.

**Continua Design Guidelines (CDG):** The PCHAlliance publishes and promotes the global adoption of standards and the implementation guidelines that unleash the massive amounts of medical-grade data that enables a more holistic perspective. Commercial-ready software enables the rapid integration of these standards into your product. A conformity assessment program verifies that the standards have been properly and uniformly implemented.

**Cybersecurity:** the protection of computer systems and networks from information disclosure, theft of or damage to their hardware, software, or electronic data, as well as from the disruption or misdirection of the services they provide.

**Data Encryption:** the process of encoding information. This process converts the original representation of the information, known as plaintext, into an alternative form known as ciphertext. Ideally, only authorized parties can decipher a ciphertext back to plaintext and access the original information. Encryption does not itself prevent interference but denies the intelligible content to a would-be interceptor. Modern encryption schemes utilize the concepts of public-key and symmetric-key. Examples of data encryption methods used to encrypt data in transit and at rest are AES-256 and TLS 2.0.

**Electrocardiogram (ECG or EKG):** a record or display of a person's heartbeat produced by electrocardiography.

**Electrocardiography (ECG or EKG):** the process of producing an electrocardiogram. It is an electrogram of the heart which is a graph of voltage versus time of the electrical activity of the heart using electrodes placed on the skin. These electrodes detect the small electrical changes that are a consequence of cardiac muscle depolarization followed by repolarization during each cardiac cycle (heartbeat).

**Electroencephalography (EEG):** a method to record an electrogram of the electrical activity on the scalp that has been shown to represent the macroscopic activity of the surface layer of the brain underneath. It is typically non-invasive, with the electrodes placed along the scalp.

**Electronic Health Record (EHR):** the systematized collection of patient and population health data/information that is electronically stored in a digital format. These records can be shared across different healthcare settings. Records are shared through network-connected, enterprise-wide information systems or other information networks and exchanges.

**Electrodermal activity (EDA):** the property of the human body that causes continuous variation in the electrical characteristics of the skin. Historically, EDA has also been known as skin conductance, galvanic skin response (GSR), electrodermal response (EDR), psycho-galvanic reflex (PGR), skin conductance response (SCR), sympathetic skin response (SSR), and skin conductance level (SCL). The long history of research into the active and passive electrical properties of the skin by a variety of disciplines has resulted in an excess of names, now standardized to electrodermal activity (EDA) or Transcutaneous Electrical Nerve Stimulation (TENS).

**Electromyogram (EMG):** is the measurement of the signal that activates muscles.

**Emergency Department (ED):** An emergency department (ED), also known as an accident and emergency department (A&E), emergency room (ER), emergency ward (EW), or casualty department, is a medical treatment facility specializing in emergency medicine, the acute care of patients who present without prior appointment; either by their own means or by that of an ambulance.

**Fast Health Interoperability Responses (FHIR):** a standard describing data formats and elements (known as "resources") and an application programming interface (API) for exchanging electronic health records (EHR). The standard was created by the Health Level Seven International (HL7) healthcare standards organization. One of its goals is to facilitate interoperability between legacy healthcare systems, to make it easy to provide healthcare information to healthcare providers and individuals on a wide variety of devices from computers to tablets to cell phones, and to allow third-party application developers to provide medical applications which can be easily integrated into existing systems. hl7.org/fhir is a next-generation standards framework created by HL7. FHIR combines the best features of HL7's v2, HL7 v3, and CDA product lines while leveraging the latest web standards and applying a tight focus on implementation. FHIR solutions are built from a set of modular components called "Resources." These resources can easily be assembled into working systems that solve real-world clinical and administrative problems at a fraction of the price of existing alternatives.

**Food and Drug Administration (FDA):** a federal agency of the Department of Health and Human Services. The FDA is responsible for protecting and promoting public health through the control and supervision of food safety, tobacco products, dietary supplements, prescription and over-the-counter pharmaceutical drugs (medications), vaccines, biopharmaceuticals, blood transfusions, medical devices, electromagnetic radiation emitting devices (ERED), cosmetics, animal foods and feed[4], and veterinary products.

**Frequency:** the number of occurrences of a repeating event per unit of time. It is also occasionally referred to as temporal frequency to emphasize the contrast to spatial frequency, and ordinary frequency to emphasize the contrast to angular frequency. Frequency is measured in hertz (Hz), which is equal to one event per second. The period is the duration of time of one cycle in a repeating event, so the period is the reciprocal of the frequency.

**Gateways:** a piece of networking hardware or software used in telecommunications networks that allows data to flow from one discrete network to another. Gateways are distinct from routers or switches in that they communicate using more than one protocol to connect multiple networks and can operate at any of the seven layers of the open systems interconnection model (OSI).

**The Global Positioning System (GPS):** originally Navstar, GPS is a satellite-based radionavigation system owned by the United States government and operated by the United States Space Force. It is one of the global navigation satellite systems (GNSS) that provides geolocation and time information to a GPS receiver anywhere on or near the Earth where there is an unobstructed line of sight to four or more GPS satellites. Obstacles such as mountains and buildings can block the relatively weak GPS signals.

**United States Department of Health and Human Services (HHS):**
a cabinet-level executive branch department of the US federal
government created to protect the health of all Americans and
provide essential human services. Its motto is "Improving the
health, safety, and well-being of America." HHS is administered
by the Secretary of Health and Human Services, who is appointed
by the president with the advice and consent of the United States
Senate.

**Health Information Exchanges (HIE):** mobilize healthcare information electronically across organizations within a region, community, or hospital system. Participants in data exchange are called
the aggregate Health Information Networks (HIN). In practice, the
term HIE may also refer to the health information organization
(HIO) that facilitates the exchange. HIE provides the capability to
electronically move clinical information among different healthcare
information systems. The goal of HIE is to facilitate access to and
retrieval of clinical data to provide safer and more timely, efficient,
effective, and equitable patient-centered care, which may also be
useful to public health authorities in analyses of the health of the
population.

**Health Insurance Portability and Accountability Act of 1996
(HIPAA):** a United States federal statute enacted by the 104th United
States Congress and signed into law by President Bill Clinton on
August 21, 1996. It modernized the flow of healthcare information,
stipulates how personally identifiable information maintained by the
healthcare and healthcare insurance industries should be protected
from fraud and theft, and addressed some limitations on healthcare
insurance coverage. It generally prohibits healthcare providers and
healthcare businesses, called covered entities, from disclosing private
information to anyone other than a patient and the patient's authorized representatives.

**Health Level Seven (HL7):** a set of international standards for transfer of
clinical and administrative data between software applications used
by various healthcare providers. These standards focus on the application layer, which is "layer 7" in the OSI model. The HL7 standards
are produced by Health Level Seven International, an international
standards organization, and are adopted by other standards-
issuing bodies such as American National Standards Institute and
International Organization for Standardization.

**IEEE:** the Institute of Electrical and Electronic Engineers, an organization that represents electrical and electronic engineers and develops standards in this field.

**Interoperability:** two or more systems use common data formats and communication protocols and can communicate with each other; they exhibit syntactic interoperability. FHIR, XML, and SQL are examples of common data formats and protocols. Lower-level data formats also contribute to syntactic interoperability, ensuring that alphabetical characters are stored in the same ASCII or Unicode format in all the communicating systems.

**Integrating the Healthcare Enterprise (IHE):** an organization whose aim is to improve how electronic patient information is shared among healthcare systems and, by doing so, to make sure that current and accurate data is readily available to both patients and healthcare professionals. IHE has developed technical frameworks that define how to process healthcare events, how data is shared, how security is handled, how audit records are generated, and how components interact with one another.

**Information and Communication Technology (ICT):** is an extensional term for information technology (IT) that stresses the role of unified communications and the integration of telecommunications (telephone lines and wireless signals) and computers, as well as necessary enterprise software, middleware, storage and audiovisual, that enable users to access, store, transmit, understand, and manipulate information.

**Information Technology (IT):** the use of computers to create, process, store, and exchange all kinds of electronic data and information. IT is typically used within the context of business operations as opposed to personal or entertainment technologies.

**Infrared (IR):** sometimes called infrared light, is electromagnetic radiation (EMR) with wavelengths longer than those of visible light. It is therefore invisible to the human eye. IR is generally understood to encompass wavelengths from the nominal red edge of the visible spectrum around 700 nanometers (frequency 430 THz), to 1 millimeter (300 GHz). Infrared radiation is emitted or absorbed by molecules when they change their rotational-vibrational movements. It excites vibrational modes in a molecule through a change in the dipole moment, making it a useful frequency range for studying these energy states for molecules of the proper symmetry.

**Intensive Care Unit (ICU):** also known as an intensive therapy unit or intensive treatment unit (ITU) or critical care unit (CCU), is a special department of a hospital or healthcare facility that provides intensive care medicine. Intensive care units cater to patients with severe or life-threatening illnesses and injuries, which require constant care, close supervision from life support equipment, vital sign monitors, and medication in order to ensure normal bodily functions. They are staffed by highly trained physicians, nurses, and respiratory therapists who specialize in caring for critically ill patients.

**International Organization for Standardization (ISO):** an international standard-setting body composed of representatives from various national standards organizations. Founded on February 23, 1947, the organization develops and publishes worldwide technical, industrial, and commercial standards. It is headquartered in Geneva, Switzerland, and works in 165 countries. Use of the standards aids in the creation of products and services that are safe, reliable, and of good quality. The standards help businesses increase productivity while minimizing errors and waste.

**Internet Service Provider (ISP):** an organization that provides many different services for accessing, using, or participating on the Internet. Internet service providers can be organized in various forms, such as commercial, community-owned, non-profit, or otherwise privately owned. Internet services typically provided by ISPs can include Internet access, Internet transit, domain name registration, web hosting, Usenet service, and colocation.

**Local Area Network (LAN):** a computer network that interconnects computers within a limited area such as a residence, school, laboratory, hospital, university campus, or office building.[1] By contrast, a wide area network (WAN) not only covers a larger geographic distance but also generally involves leased telecommunication circuits. Ethernet and Wi-Fi are the two most common technologies in use for local area networks. Historical network technologies include ARCNET, Token Ring, and AppleTalk.

**Long Term Evolution Machine Type Communication (LTE-MTC/LTE-M):** includes eMTC (enhanced Machine Type Communication): a type of low power wide area network (LPWAN) radio technology standard developed by 3GPP to enable a wide range of cellular devices and services (specifically, for machine-to-machine and Internet of Things applications). Other 3GPP IoT technologies include NB-IoT

and EC-GSM-IoT. The advantage of LTE-M over NB-IoT is its com-
paratively higher data rate, mobility, and voice over the network, but
it requires more bandwidth, is more costly, and cannot be put in to
guard band frequency band for now.

**LoRa:** a proprietary, chirp spread spectrum radio modulation technology for
LPWAN used by LoRaWAN, Haystack Technologies, and Symphony
Link.

**Low Power Wide Area Network (LPWAN):** or low-power wide-area
(LPWA) network or low-power network (LPN) is a type of wireless
telecommunication wide-area network designed to allow long-range
communications at a low bit rate among things (connected objects),
such as sensors operated on a battery. The low power, low bit rate,
and intended use distinguish this type of network from a wireless
WAN that is designed to connect users or businesses and carry more
data, using more power. The LPWAN data rate ranges from 0.3 kbit/s
to 50 kbit/s per channel.

**Mesh Network:** a local network topology in which the infrastructure nodes
(i.e., bridges, switches, and other infrastructure devices) connect
directly, dynamically, and non-hierarchically to as many other nodes
as possible and cooperate with one another to efficiently route data
from/to clients. This lack of dependency on one node allows for every
node to participate in the relay of information. Mesh networks dynamically self-organize and self-configure, which can reduce installation
overhead. The ability to self-configure enables dynamic distribution of
workloads, particularly in the event a few nodes should fail. This in
turn contributes to fault-tolerance and reduced maintenance costs.

**Micro-Electrical Mechanical System (MEMS):** a technology that in its
most general form can be defined as miniaturized mechanical and
electro-mechanical elements (i.e., devices and structures) that are
made using the techniques of microfabrication. The critical physical
dimensions of MEMS devices can vary from well below one micron
on the lower end of the dimensional spectrum, all the way to several millimeters. Likewise, the types of MEMS devices can vary from
relatively simple structures having no moving elements, to extremely
complex electromechanical systems with multiple moving elements
under the control of integrated microelectronics. The one main cri-
terion of MEMS is that there are at least some elements having some
sort of mechanical functionality whether or not these elements can
move.

**Narrowband Internet of Things (NB-IoT):** a low-power wide-area net-work (LPWAN) radio technology standard developed by 3GPP for cellular devices and services. Other 3GPP IoT technologies include eMTC (enhanced Machine-Type Communication) and EC-GSM-IoT. NB-IoT focuses specifically on indoor coverage, low cost, long battery life, and high connection density.

**National Institute of Standards and Technology (NIST):** a physical sciences laboratory and non-regulatory agency of the United States Department of Commerce. Its mission is to promote American inno-vation and industrial competitiveness. NIST's activities are organized into laboratory programs that include nanoscale science and technol-ogy, engineering, information technology, neutron research, material measurement, and physical measurement.

**Near Field Communication (NFC):** a set of communication protocols for communication between two electronic devices over a distance of four cm (1–1/2 in) or less. NFC offers a low-speed connection with simple setup that can be used to bootstrap more capable wireless connections. NFC devices can act as electronic identity documents and keycards. They are used in contactless payment systems and allow mobile payment replacing or supplementing systems such as credit cards and electronic ticket smart cards.

**The Office of the National Coordinator for Health Information Technology (ONC):** a staff division of the Office of the Secretary, within the US Department of Health and Human Services. ONC leads national health IT efforts, charged as the principal federal entity to coordinate nationwide efforts to implement and use the most advanced health information technology and the electronic exchange of health information.

**Peripheral oxygen saturation (SpO2):** an estimation of the oxygen satu-ration level usually measured with a pulse oximeter device using a PPG sensor.

**The Personal Connected Health Alliance (PCHAlliance):** is working to advance patient/consumer-centered health, wellness, and disease pre-vention. The Alliance mobilizes a coalition of stakeholders to realize the full potential of personal connected health.

**Personal Health Device Group:** within the context of the ISO/IEEE 11073 family of standards for device communication, this standard estab-lishes a normative definition of the communication between per-sonal basic electrocardiograph (ECG) devices and managers (e.g., cell phones, personal computers, personal health appliances, and set-top boxes) in a manner that enables plug-and-play interoperability.

**Photoplethysmography (PPG) sensor:** an optically obtained plethysmogram that can be used to detect blood volume changes and oxygen saturation in the microvascular bed of tissue.

**Pulse Oximeter:** a medical device that provides a noninvasive method for monitoring a person's oxygen saturation.

**Radio Frequency Identification (RFID):** uses electromagnetic fields to automatically identify and track tags attached to objects. An RFID system consists of a tiny radio transponder, a radio receiver, and a transmitter. When triggered by an electromagnetic interrogation pulse from a nearby RFID reader device, the tag transmits digital data, usually an identifying inventory number, back to the reader. This number can be used to track inventory goods. Passive tags are powered by energy from the RFID reader's interrogating radio waves. Active tags are powered by a battery and thus can be read at a greater range from the RFID reader, up to hundreds of meters. Unlike a barcode, the tag does not need to be within the line of sight of the reader, so it may be embedded in the tracked object. RFID is one method of automatic identification and data capture (AIDC).

**Rapid eye movement sleep (REM sleep or REMS):** a unique phase of sleep in mammals and birds, characterized by random rapid movement of the eyes, accompanied by low muscle tone throughout the body, and the propensity of the sleeper to dream vividly.

**Remote Patient Monitoring (RPM):** a technology to enable monitoring of patients outside of conventional clinical settings, such as in the home or in a remote area, which may increase access to care and decrease healthcare delivery costs. RPM involves the constant remote care of patients by their physicians, often to track physical symptoms, chronic conditions, or post-hospitalization rehabilitation.

**RTLS or Real-time Locating Systems:** also known as real-time tracking systems, are used to automatically identify and track the location of objects or people in real time, usually within a building or other contained area. Wireless RTLS tags are attached to objects or worn by people, and in most RTLS, fixed reference points receive wireless signals from tags to determine their location.

**Sensor:** a device, module, machine, or subsystem whose purpose is to detect events or changes in its environment and send the information to other electronics, frequently a computer processor. A sensor is always used with other electronics.

**Sigfox:** a French global network operator founded in 2010 that builds wireless networks to connect low-power objects such as electricity meters and smartwatches, which need to be continuously on and emitting small amounts of data.

**SIM Card:** also known as subscriber identity module or subscriber identification module (SIM), is an integrated circuit running a card operating system (COS) that is intended to securely store the international mobile subscriber identity (IMSI) number and its related key, which are used to identify and authenticate subscribers on mobile telephony devices (such as mobile phones and computers). It is also possible to store contact information on many SIM cards. SIM cards are always used on GSM phones; for CDMA phones, they are needed only for LTE-capable handsets. SIM cards can also be used in satellite phones, smartwatches, computers, or cameras.

**Smart Home:** a home automation system that will monitor and/or control home attributes such as lighting, climate, entertainment systems, and appliances. It may also include home security such as access control and alarm systems. When connected to the Internet, home devices are an important constituent of the Internet of Things ("IoT"). Many RPM devices are IoT compatible. A home automation system typically connects controlled devices to a central smart home hub (sometimes called a "gateway").

**Smartphone:** a portable device that combines mobile telephone and computing functions into one unit. They are distinguished from feature phones by their stronger hardware capabilities and extensive mobile operating systems, which facilitate wider software, internet (including web browsing over mobile broadband), and multimedia functionality (including music, video, cameras, and gaming), alongside core phone functions such as voice calls and text messaging.

**Smartwatch:** a wearable computer in the form of a watch; modern smartwatches provide a local touchscreen interface for daily use, while an associated smartphone app provides for management and telemetry (such as long-term biomonitoring). While early models could perform basic tasks, such as calculations, digital time telling, translations, and game-playing. Since 2010 smartwatches have more general functionality closer to smartphones, including mobile apps, a mobile operating system, and WiFi/Bluetooth connectivity.

**Software Development Kit (SDK):** a collection of software development tools in one installable package. They facilitate the creation of applications by having a compiler, debugger, and perhaps a software framework. They are normally specific to a hardware platform and operating system combination. To create applications with advanced functionalities such as advertisements and push notifications as examples. Most application software developers use specific software development kits. Some SDKs are required for developing a platform-specific app. For example, the development of an Android app on the Java platform requires a Java Development Kit. For iOS applications (apps), the iOS SDK is required.

**Telehealth:** the distribution of health-related services and information via electronic information and telecommunication technologies. It allows long-distance patient and clinician contact, care, advice, reminders, education, intervention, monitoring, and remote admissions.

**Telemedicine:** is sometimes used as a synonym or is used in a more limited sense to describe remote clinical services, such as diagnosis and monitoring. When rural settings, lack of transport, a lack of mobility, conditions due to outbreaks, epidemics or pandemics, decreased funding, or a lack of staff restrict access to care, telehealth may bridge the gap as well as provide distance-learning; meetings, supervision, and presentations between practitioners; online information and health data management and healthcare system integration.

**Ultrasound:** sound waves with frequencies higher than the upper audible limit of human hearing. Ultrasound is not different from "normal" (audible) sound in its physical properties, except that humans cannot hear it. This limit varies from person to person and is approximately 20 kilohertz (20,000 hertz) in healthy young adults. Ultrasound devices operate with frequencies from 20 kHz up to several gigahertz. Ultrasound is used in many different fields. Ultrasonic devices are used to detect objects and measure distances. Ultrasound imaging or sonography is often used in medicine.

**User Experience (UX):** how a user interacts with and experiences a product, system, or service. It includes a person's perceptions of utility, ease of use, and efficiency.

**User Interface (UI):** the space where interactions between humans and machines occur. The goal of this interaction is to allow effective operation and control of the machine from the human end, while the machine simultaneously feeds back information that aids the operators' decision-making process.

**Voice biomarkers:** represent voice data used for detecting alterations in health. The voice is a complex result of our muscles and brain working together with maximum precision. Mild or severe modifications in voice and language can be an indicator of various diseases, making vocal biomarkers a noninvasive tool for detecting and tracking these diseases.

**Wearable Technology:** also referred to as wearables, fashion technology, smartwear, tech togs, skin electronics, or fashion electronics are smart electronic devices (electronic devices with micro-controllers) that are worn close to and/or on the surface of the skin, where they detect, analyze, and transmit information concerning body signals such as vital signs, and/or ambient data and which allow in some cases immediate biofeedback to the wearer. Wearable devices such as activity trackers are an example of the Internet of Things since "things" such as electronics, software, sensors, and connectivity are effectors that enable objects to exchange data (including data quality) through the internet with a manufacturer, operator, and/or other connected devices, without requiring human intervention.

**Wide Area Network (WAN):** a telecommunications network that extends over a large geographic area for the primary purpose of computer networking. Wide area networks are often established with leased telecommunication circuits. Businesses, as well as schools and government entities, use wide area networks to relay data to staff, students, clients, buyers, and suppliers from various locations across the world. In essence, this mode of telecommunication allows a business to effectively carry out its daily function regardless of location. The Internet may be considered a WAN. WANs are used to connect LANs and other types of networks together so that users and computers in one location can communicate with users and computers in other locations. Many WANs are built for one organization and are private. Others, built by Internet service providers, provide connections from an organization's LAN to the Internet.

**Wi-Fi:** a family of wireless network protocols, based on the IEEE 802.11 family of standards, which are commonly used for local area networking of devices and Internet access, allowing nearby digital devices to exchange data by radio waves. These are the most widely used computer networks in the world, used globally in home and small office networks to link desktop and laptop computers, tablet computers, smartphones, smart TVs, printers, and smart speakers together and to a wireless router to connect them to the Internet, and in wireless access points in public places like coffee shops, hotels, libraries, and airports to provide the public Internet access for mobile devices.

**Wireless Communication or Wireless:** the transfer of information between two or more points that do not use an electrical conductor as a medium by which to perform the transfer. The most common wireless technologies use radio waves. With radio waves, intended distances can be short, such as a few meters for Bluetooth or as far as millions of kilometers for deep-space radio communications. It encompasses various types of fixed, mobile, and portable applications, including two-way radios, cellular telephones, personal digital assistants (PDAs), and wireless networking. Other examples of applications of radio wireless technology include GPS units, garage door openers, wireless computer mouse, keyboards and headsets, headphones, radio receivers, satellite television, broadcast television, and cordless telephones. Somewhat less common methods of achieving wireless communications include the use of other electromagnetic wireless technologies, such as light, magnetic, or electric fields or the use of sound.

**Zigbee:** an IEEE 802.15.4-based specification for a suite of high-level communication protocols used to create personal area networks with small, low-power digital radios, such as for home automation, medical device data collection, and other low-power low-bandwidth needs, designed for small-scale projects which need wireless connection. Hence, Zigbee is a low-power, low data rate, and close proximity (i.e., personal area) wireless ad hoc network. The technology defined by the Zigbee specification is intended to be simpler and less expensive than other wireless personal area networks (WPANs), such as Bluetooth or more general wireless networking such as Wi-Fi.

Many definitions came from Wikipedia.

# Index

Note: Page numbers in *italics* indicate figures; page numbers in **bold** indicate tables.

Printed in the United States
by Baker & Taylor Publisher Services